PROSODIC PHRASE IN SPOKEN CZECH

JAN **VOLÍN**
PAVEL **ŠTURM**
RADEK **SKARNITZL**
TOMÁŠ **BOŘIL**

CHARLES UNIVERSITY
KAROLINUM PRESS, 2024

KAROLINUM PRESS
Karolinum Press is a publishing department of Charles University
Ovocný trh 560/5, 116 36 Prague 1, Czech Republic
www.karolinum.cz
© Jan Volín, Pavel Šturm, Radek Skarnitzl, Tomáš Bořil, 2024
Set and printed in the Czech Republic by Karolinum Press
Layout by Jan Šerých
First edition

A catalogue record for this book is available from the National Library of the Czech Republic.

ISBN 978-80-246-5798-1
ISBN 978-80-246-5827-8 (pdf)
ISBN 978-80-246-5828-5 (epub)

The original manuscript was reviewed by Alice J. Henderson (Université Grenoble Alpes, France) and Tomáš Hoskovec (University of South Bohemia in České Budějovice, Czech Republic).

CONTENTS

Foreword ---- **7**

1. SPEECH PROSODY ---- **9**
1.1 Rationale ---- **10**
1.2 Defining prosody by form and function ---- **13**
1.3 Description of speech prosody ---- **19**

2. PROSODIC UNITS ---- **25**
2.1 Utterance ---- **26**
2.2 Phonoparagraph and turn ---- **29**
2.3 Prosodic phrase ---- **30**
2.4 Accent group, stress group, foot ---- **34**
2.5 Syllable ---- **36**

3. ANALYZED MATERIAL ---- **39**
3.1 A general note on terms ---- **40**
3.2 Poetry reciting ---- **42**
3.3 Newsreading ---- **43**
3.4 Storytelling ---- **43**
3.5 Pre-processing ---- **44**

4. PROSODIC PHRASE IN CONTEMPORARY CZECH ---- **47**
4.1 Prosodic phrase structurally ---- **48**
    4.1.1 Phrase length ---- **49**
    4.1.2 Stress group length ---- **56**
    4.1.3 Anacrusis ---- **58**
    4.1.4 Monosyllabic stress groups ---- **61**
    4.1.5 Discussion ---- **64**
4.2 Prosodic phrase acoustically ---- **66**
    4.2.1 Fundamental frequency ---- **67**
    4.2.2 Intensity ---- **73**
    4.2.3 Duration ---- **80**
    4.2.4 Voice quality ---- **86**
    4.2.5 Discussion ---- **90**
4.3 Prosodic phrase syntactically ---- **93**
    4.3.1 Theoretical underpinning ---- **93**
    4.3.2 Sentence ---- **94**
    4.3.3 Subject-predicate boundary ---- **98**

5. PROSODIC PHRASE PERCEPTUALLY ---- 107
5.1 Perceptual cues to prosodic phrasing ---- **108**
5.2 Experiment on cue weighting in Czech ---- **111**
    5.2.1 Material and methods ---- **112**
    5.2.2 Results and discussion ---- **114**
5.3 Prosodic phrasing and cognition ---- **118**
    5.3.1 Neurolinguistic correlates of prosodic phrasing ---- **118**
    5.3.2 Memory retention and other cognitive benefits ---- **120**
5.4 Experiment on memory recall in Czech ---- **121**
    5.4.1 Material and methods ---- **122**
    5.4.2 Results and discussion ---- **123**
5.5 Conclusion ---- **127**

6. STOCHASTIC MODELLING OF PHRASE BOUNDARIES ---- 129

    References ---- **137**
    Subject index ---- **145**

FOREWORD

The monograph *Prosodic Phrase in Spoken Czech*, which you are beginning to read, has been dreamt of for decades. Thirty years ago, the then Director of the Institute of Phonetics in Prague advertised her personal plans for such a book. She claimed that the topic of prosodic structure was undeniably interesting, attractive even outside phonetics, and, quite importantly, there was absence of anything in this vein for the Czech language. Informal discussions at various academic gatherings have confirmed that a treatise of this sort was needed not only by phoneticians, but also by many other people who were interested in the sound patterns of Czech, whether for technological use in speech synthesis and automatic speech recognition or for didactic, forensic, therapeutic and other purposes. Overwhelmed with other duties, she never wrote the book.

The current authors joined their capacities to materialize the plans, at least partially. Although they definitely aspired to produce a useful treatise, they were not motivated by any specific technological applications. Those have grown dominant across scientific activities far and wide: commercialized societies have become reluctant to see the sheer joy of discovery as a true value. Yet, the desire to discover and the ability to revisit existing knowledge reach above and beyond consumerism. How magnificent it would be to replace the current plundering of the Earth's wealth with admiration for it! The authors of the present book believe that the complexity of every aspect of our lives deserves thorough study, and that the resulting knowledge should be shared.

Naturally, there needs to be demand for knowledge. The trouble is that when it comes to language, everybody 'has an opinion'. All humans typically use language to communicate, and many believe, by extension, that they are experts on language even if they never trained anything but spelling rules. One has to wonder if there is any scientific field more plagued with dilettantism and ignorance than linguistics.

These words sound perhaps a bit too harsh. Not everyone chooses ignorance willingly and deliberately. And it is only very recently that people have started accepting the fact that there is a massive gap between what we are able to capture by our limited conscious circuitry and what our whole brains really do. The way we are currently able to describe language analytically is not the way language really works. Recent research in adaptive, implicit thinking has brought evidence that we do not realize how we function: how we process what we sense and how we plan our actions. Our consciousness cannot capture what we really feel before it is censored by various mental mechanisms. Yet, all this is extremely relevant to linguistics, and this is also why we currently witness a powerful shift from speculative to empirical methods.

Less self-satisfaction and more patient work are becoming typical for linguists. For instance, old introductory manuals used to amaze students with the claim that a finite number of small elements can be used to create an infinite number of utterances. We can leave the practical impact of this dazzling claim aside, but one thing is clear. It obscures the fact that people do not use infinite numbers of utterances in their everyday lives. This is because what we communicate is strictly grounded in what we live. Huge numbers are not infinity. The infinitely rich inner world of an immortal being is one of the pompous anthropocentric myths.

Therefore, let us focus with modesty on limited samples of true attempts to communicate. The seemingly pleonastic word 'spoken' in the title of this book was used purposefully: we wanted to emphasize that we do not estimate prosodic phrasing from written text as some scholars did in the past. Neither do we use invented contextless sentences where the communicative intent of speakers may be dubious or completely absent. On the other hand, we do not dare to use recordings of spontaneous conversations as yet: those are difficult to obtain legally, and they are difficult to analyze in our current linguistic framework. We opted for spoken texts that are produced with legitimate communicative intents and, yet, provide manageable and dependable data. We hope this approach may help us as authors and you as readers to find a way from biased or circular discussions towards the joy of discovery adequate to the times we live in.

Prague, August 2023
The Authors

1. SPEECH PROSODY

1.1 RATIONALE

The value of language communication has been most probably appreciated already in pre-history. Even before people started recording their thoughts, important contracts, laws or observations in writing, they must have realized how important their speech behaviour was. From sheer admiration for the power of speech (often explicated as a magnificent gift from gods) people gradually moved to systematic observations, disciplined descriptions, and rigorous experimenting, i.e., to scientific treatment of speech. This approach embraced writing as well and, inevitably, the system that governs both of these communication means – language.

There is currently little opposition to the claim that language communication should be studied scientifically. Even though language use is omnipresent and quite pervasive in our everyday lives, when considered thoroughly it can hardly be seen as trivial. Unfortunately, there is still the awkward legacy of the past, by which linguistics is sorted into 'less precise' or 'less scientific' disciplines. However, this primordial figment is nowadays either just a superficial feeling of someone who has no capacity for deeper critical thinking or an unfair excuse in the relentless fight for resources in the current system of science financing. Be that as it may, modern linguistics can offer very interesting insights into the functioning of language. Phonetics, which is ultimately by its goals a linguistic discipline, has been doing so beyond any doubt.

One of the serious problems with the credibility of the past linguistics was the claim that human language is 'utterly unique' and, therefore, can be explained only from itself. This type of mysticism, within which scholars *a priori* decide not to see any connections with other communicative systems and not to seek any compatibility with other scientific disciplines, was self-destructive. Fortunately, it was prevalently abandoned before it made linguistics completely socially irrelevant. Most current linguists do not shy away from testing their hypotheses with methods that originated in psychology, neurophysiology, ethology, sociology, etc. In addition, a powerful boost to linguistic theories has been provided by the increased possibilities of cross-linguistic research.

A brief but patent example of the above-described developments can be found in the following quote: "… there are differences in delta responses across languages due to the different usage of stress. In English and German, for example, phrasal responses are emphasized but in French, syllabicity remains dominant." (Ghitza, Giraud & Poeppel, 2013). The authors carry out cross-language comparisons and they use neurophysiological correlates of perceptual processes. The underlying message indicates that prosodic structure is of relevance. The phrasal responses mentioned in the quote are especially relevant to the chief topic of the present book. They point to a speech unit that, under various names and with various attributes across languages, seems to be always somehow present in the hierarchical structure: the PROSODIC PHRASE.

Already in 2001, Chafe observed that prosodic phrases in his corpus of conversational speech were "typically one to two seconds long", which to him was about the span of active consciousness. He also proposed semi-active consciousness for contextual information, but claimed that attention can only be devoted to smaller chunks of information (Chafe, 2001: 675). According to him, this 'information packaging' is essential for smooth speech processing by interacting individuals.

Two decades later, LaCroix and her colleagues listed a large number of studies that had resulted in the inference that "typical sentence prosody yields faster and more accurate sentence comprehension performance than atypical prosodic patterns" (LaCroix et al., 2020: 2). Their own experiment with brain-stroke patients and a group of typical language users added valid evidence to the claim.

Nowadays, it is widely accepted that division of larger stretches of speech into prosodic phrases is critical for effortless mental processing and, ultimately, even for correct recovery of intended meanings of spoken texts (be it the representational, conative, or affective components of the communicated messages). Individuals who intend to talk about objects and events of the surrounding world must always select only a limited choice of aspects to talk about at a time, while ignoring or backgrounding others. This is because taking all possible observables into account at once would be beyond human cognitive capacities and, also, beyond the potentials of natural language. Prosodic structure contributes to the process of focusing the addressee's attention on those aspects of reality that need to be communicated at the given moment, and provides a particular perspective on the state of affairs (in line with the personal intents of the speaker). Prosodic phrases – the central object of study in this monograph – belong among the devices that speakers use to guide listeners through spoken texts to desired conclusions.

From today's perspective, it would be quite naïve to imagine that listeners analyze linear flows of small units (phonemes, syllables) and glue them in their mind together to compose units that are meaningful. Phonemes and syllables need to be seen as mere features of meaningful items, and their qualities and positions only serve to recognize those meaningful objects as wholes. As long as these wholes fit into the given situation, they do not need to be analyzed into their parts. People do not have to focus on the exact qualities and the precise positions of 'features'; in fact, if they did, speech communication could not have developed into the fast process that it is. Recent development in this research area suggests quite convincingly that we even do not necessarily assemble our utterances from individual words. There is evidence from various sources (e.g., young infants, aphasic patients, motoric patterns in typing, eye movement in reading, etc.) pointing to the use of MULTI-WORD UNITS (MWU) and the holistic storage of those in our brains (Lin, 2018: 48 and 53; Ellis, 2003: 75). It is hypothesized that speakers provide various cues about the boundaries of such meaningful units as they plan their utterances in them.

Although the above are various general conclusions based on empirical findings, Kohler emphasizes that there are profound differences in speakers' proficiency concerning phrasing (Kohler, 2018: 147). In other words, speakers are more or less adept at grouping words together in a way that is transparent and easy to follow for listeners. Kohler links the dexterity in prosodic phrasing to the more general cognitive skill of argumentation and perhaps even logical thinking. He demonstrates how, first, the placement of a boundary and, second, the relative strength of a boundary (expressed by means of prosodic markers) may influence the perceived information structure in the spoken text. The past decades produced quite a large number of studies that experiment with such semantic ambiguities. For instance, the following string of words forms an ordinary Czech sentence:

Czech:	Dá se	tam	volat	v sobotu	a	v neděli	večer
English:	It's possible	there	to telephone	on Saturday	and	on Sunday	evening

We demonstrate two different prosodic boundary placements that result in two different interpretations of the proper time for making the telephone call. If the phrasal boundary is placed as follows:

Dá se tam volat ‖ v sobotu a v neděli večer,

the intended meaning is that the phone call is possible on both days always in the evening.

On the other hand, if the phrasal break is in the following position:

Dá se tam volat v sobotu ‖ a v neděli večer,

the phone call is possible the whole day on Saturday, but on Sunday only in the evening.

Of course, it would be unwise to restrict linguistics only to such ambiguities. Even if the meaning is clear, but difficult to understand, language communication suffers. Excessive effort on the part of the recipient projects far beyond just a single utterance meaning. Struggling recipients are less likely to cooperate with the speaker, less likely to even trust the speaker, and unlikely to proliferate any positive feelings both within and outside the conversation.

Whether we focus on completely misleading outcomes or just cumbersome speech processing, it is unquestionable that the prosodic phrase is an important element of prosodic structure and of communication in general. As such, it deserves attention of anyone who is interested in human language. This book is our response to the demand.

1.2 DEFINING PROSODY BY FORM AND FUNCTION

Define your terms if you wish to converse with me, an enlightened thinker once allegedly said. Indeed, it is impossible to discuss problems with someone who ascribes unknown meanings to his or her words. Ideas can only be effectively examined if the discussants follow a common path, if one person's reaction to the other person's thought matches as much as possible the intended meaning. In other words, ideas and reactions to them must 'meet in a shared space'. There is a lot to discuss in the field of prosody research. What is prosody of speech, then?

This is a question that researchers in prosody do not particularly like. Not that it is uninteresting. On the contrary, if discussed by experts it often leads to exciting interactions. However, people who ask the question in this simple form usually expect a simple answer. Such an answer, regrettably, does not exist. If we try to provide an uncomplicated answer, substantial parts of the truth may remain unspoken.

Three types of definitions are heard most often: definition by negation, definition by parallel, and definition by listing.

The definition by negation is very common in communities that use alphabetic orthographies. In such communities, young children discover very early in their lives that individual letters of their alphabet refer to specific little sounds. Enormous care devoted to these little sounds at schools (even at pre-school establishments or within families) results in the idea that language consists only of those. They are highly activated in people's minds, while the larger sound phenomena remain produced or perceived with little explicit awareness. Relying on the common knowledge of little sounds represented by letters of the alphabet, speech prosody is then explained as 'everything in speech that is not represented by the letters of the alphabet, e.g., by phones or segmental phonemes'. (It should be added that this 'everything' is meant as communicatively functional sound phenomena.)

The definition by parallel exploits another known concept: that of music. Since music plays a very important role in human communities, it can be put forward as analogous with speech. Prosody is then explained as an aggregate of all the phenomena that speech shares with music: melody, rhythm, tempo, timbre and loudness.

Definition by listing skips the analogy with music and relies on the common knowledge of prosodic phenomena. The list might then be virtually the same as the above, i.e., melody, rhythm, tempo, voice quality patterns and distribution of loudness, or it might list some of the partial phenomena on their own. This is often the case of stress, which can be studied on its own but is an essential part of rhythm.

An interesting approach is taken by Nespor and Vogel (1983), who begin their consideration of what prosody is by listing various prosodic units. Their list comprises: "rhyme, syllable, foot, phonological word, phonological phrase, intonational phrase, and utterance" (Nespor & Vogel, 1983: 123). At this point, we can leave aside the question whether the syllabic rhyme (referred to as RIME here; see Section 2.5) is too artificial and whether prosody forms any structures above the utterance. What needs to be noticed is that by listing these units, Nespor and Vogel do not feel any further need to define what prosody is. They say that whatever happens within these units and is explained with reference to these units is prosodic. That is a combination of listing and implicit negation, which leads to a conclusion that anything above the segment is prosodic.

There are scholars who may claim that certain prosodic phenomena are only supralexical. This claim may simplify certain definitions but ultimately leads to trouble. On the one hand, it can differentiate the prosodic from the suprasegmental, for whatever reason felt as practical. On the other hand, if lexical stress can be materialized through melody (which it obviously can) and melody is ousted into the supralexical domain, we are trapped. However, if we realize that the natural use of language is actually supralexical (and this cannot be contradicted by the existence of one-word utterances), then the whole argument becomes quite unattractive. Indeed, we typically speak and write in utterances (see Section 2.1).

At this point, we could perhaps mention a colourful suggestion by Nick Ellis: "If words are the atoms of language function, then construction grammar provides the molecular level of analysis" (Ellis, 2003: 65). To elaborate on this figure, we could ascribe the phonemic level to atoms (and distinctive features to elementary particles), morphemes would be molecules, words could be cells, and utterances complex organs. Texts would then constitute organisms. Whether this simile is helpful or, on the contrary, confusing, can be decided by each reader individually. In any case, the prosody of speech (which we automatically project into written texts when reading) helps us to make sense of the intricate structures.

The last sentence of the preceding paragraph already invokes functions of prosody. Although it is easier to explain what speech prosody is by its appearance (i.e., form), the definition by function should be attempted as well. In the end, it is the function of things that makes them valuable.

In short, prosody serves to communicate meanings. This statement, however, is too vague and applies to segmental phonemes as well. Yet, even within this short proposition, there is a point to emphasize: linguistic functions should always be related to communication. Thus, if an author claims that the function of prosody is to create prominences and breaks, it is only true in the very general sense assigned to the word function. In the context of linguistics, however, such a statement would be misleading. Prominences and breaks are PROSODIC EVENTS or MEANS to fulfil (communicative) functions.

There have been many disparate attempts at listing the functions of prosody. They always reflect the frameworks within which their authors work and the purpose for which they were made. Ours will be no different in this sense. One of the many sources of our inspiration goes back almost a century to Karl Bühler (1934), who studied speech and language from the psychological point of view. He suggested that although the REPRESENTATIONAL COMPONENT of the meaning in language signs is the most obvious one, and hence might be considered primary, the AFFECTIVE and APPLICATIONAL COMPONENTS are nevertheless always present in utterances and, therefore, must be taken into consideration in any attempt to discuss language in more than a fragmentary manner. For the sake of presentational clarity, the general cognitive supra-function (to serve the comprehension of the intended meaning) can be organized into various categories. In the following paragraphs, we will present our understanding of the affective function, discourse function, grammatical function, sociophonetic function, aesthetic function and lexical function.

The phylogenetically oldest function is the AFFECTIVE one. Affective processes can be observed also in non-human animals. They are adaptive evaluations that according to their strength, timing, and other parameters can be classified into emotions, moods, interactive stances, attitudes, and affective personal characteristics (Scherer, 2003). The affective component of meaning is present in all utterances with greater or smaller explicitness. Humans always signal their evaluations of the topics they talk about, of the addressees, or of the situations they are in. Even the so-called neutral style (which is extremely rare in real life) displays an implicit affective component: "I don't want to share my evaluation with you". If used, it is usually to keep distance between the speaker and the recipient(s). It is sometimes claimed, for instance, that lectures are presented without affective components, but we argue that good lecturers always display their involvement in the presented issues and their feelings about various aspects of their talk. If a lecturer is disinterested or monotonous, he or she displays clear negative inner evaluations. Prosody plays a key role in signalling affective processes, hence the common phrase "It is not what you said, it is how you said it". The affective function is sometimes labelled as attitudinal and sometimes as paralinguistic. The latter term is quite unfortunate, since it cripples our understanding of what the basis of language fundamentally is. By suggesting that the "how you said it" should be relegated outside of linguistics, one would strip the language of its essential core and make linguistics dangerously detached from reality.

Bühler's 'Appell' (1934) evolved in other traditions into an illocutionary force (Austin, 1962) from which we derive the applicative or conative component of utterance meaning. It refers to what the speaker wants to achieve through speaking. The reason why certain things are uttered is not necessarily obvious, and even the speakers themselves may not know why they are using certain discourse devices. This is because they often plan their speech production implicitly and the true motivations for certain lexical, syntactic and prosodic choices may stay hidden to their conscious mind. However, it is generally presupposed that healthy individuals act purposefully, even if the purpose is not accessible to their conscious observation. What should be achieved by individual utterances is related to the DISCOURSE FUNCTION of prosody.

Since human intentions and motivations are immensely varied, the discourse function is difficult to circumscribe. In the narrow sense, it is defined as managing solely the spoken interaction. By certain prosodic forms, the speaker can express what he or she expects from the recipient. Prosody may signal a wish to receive more information, to elicit the recipient's opinion, to ask for approval, to give permission to talk, etc. The speaker does not have to use explicit words for that. Consider the following exchange.

A: You may need my ID card, though
B: OK (↗)

The expression *ok* is used for acceptance in this case, but pronouncing it with rising intonation is likely to be interpreted in the sense of *Could you explain why exactly*? Prosodic information itself performs the function of several hypothetical words.

Although this narrow understanding of discourse function seems to be currently quite common, we should still consider some wider interpretations. One of them includes the accentual capacity of prosodic cues. The fact that certain semantic components of an utterance can receive special prominence suggests a different form of discourse management. This time it is not just what to say next, but also how to think about what is being said. Prosodic means provide a functional perspective on the spoken contents (*cf.* Firbas, 1992). By accenting and deaccenting, certain words are put forward to the recipient as referring to the previous co-text or to supposedly known facts, while others are presented as new pieces of information in the given utterance.

The recipient of an utterance is led to specific mental processing of its lexical content. It is as if the speaker, apart from the individual words, said simultaneously over each part of the utterance: "This is something/someone I believe you know/expect" or "This is something/someone I believe you don't know/expect." This simultaneous work is achieved by prosody since, clearly, verbal commenting would be highly impractical or cumbersome at the very least.

To make the interpretation of the discourse function even wider would probably be too bold at this point. However, let us consider at least the direction in which it would lead. The scientific disciplines of discourse analysis (DA) and, especially, critical discourse analysis (CDA) are founded on the fact that spoken and written texts which humans produce serve to organize their communities, their institutions, their whole lives. Utterances are spoken to either maintain a certain state of affairs, or to change it. If this fact is included as a defining one into the discourse function of prosody, then it would overlap with the conative component of the communicated meanings. Apart from managing the recipient's behaviour in the speech interaction and directing his or her thoughts, it would also manage the recipient's behaviour and feelings after the interaction ends.

The danger of this wider concept lies in its vagueness. To link the prosodic cues with what a person does or thinks after receiving a spoken message would often require too much speculation, which might no longer be compatible with the current requirements on empirical research. Still, it is something that should be not only considered, but also tested. Then, perhaps, the speculative aspect may be reined in, at least to a certain extent.

The GRAMMATICAL FUNCTION of prosody seems to be much less controversial. There is a long tradition of research into correspondences between grammatical categories and prosodic structure. A well-known example is the differentiation between statements and questions, especially in languages where other markers may be missing. Czech is one of such languages: plain statements and polarity questions (also referred to as yes/no questions) may use identical strings of words. In writing, the question mark is used to disambiguate the two meanings, while in speaking there are specific melodic patterns that serve this purpose. However, the issue is far from simple since there are various types of questions and even in the case of polarity questions the grammatical function regularly combines with the affective and discourse functions; that may result in melodic patterns which deviate from those derived from abstract grammatical categories.

Apart from the grammatical type of an utterance, prosody can and often does signal the syntactic structure of longer constructions. Prosodic phrases coincide with various syntactic constituents (see also Section 2.3 and 4.3). A special case of syntactic delimitation is that of parenthetical units. When speakers want to supplement their main message with a background comment on an item within the message, they may not only separate such a comment in its own prosodic phrase, but they may also produce the phrase with faster tempo, lower loudness, lowered pitch range and possibly some other cues like greater breathiness or nasality.

The grammatical function of prosody may, in a certain sense, be also seen as related to one aspect of various word-level prominences. In many languages, prosodic prominences have been observed to differentiate between word-class groups in the lexicon or, more precisely, between the semantic supra-classes of autosemantic (content) and synsemantic (structural, function) words. This division of lexical items may be reflected by enhanced or reduced prominence, respectively; in other words, content words are often realized as more prominent (for example, louder or higher in pitch) than function words (see Section 2.4 for more detail). Again, the situation in authentic communication is complicated by the frequency of occurrence of individual words, their information status and the affective component of utterance meaning.

The SOCIOPHONETIC FUNCTION is sometimes branded as extralinguistic. Let us consider the issue. Certain prosodic markers (for instance, specific melodic patterns or voice quality features) are linked with the speaker's membership of a social group. These groups can be of different sizes and levels of abstractness (and subsequent precision in their delimitation). They may be defined geographically, culturally, economically, biologically, etc. If the speaker is unaware of their group membership while selecting forms for his or her utterance, then, indeed, the sociophonetic markers act extralinguistically. If, however, the speaker wants to suppress or emphasize his belonging to a community, then he or she uses the sociophonetic markers linguistically. This is because language is a system to communicate all sorts of meanings, not to build grammatical items. Extralinguistic or not, the sociophonetic function is definitely relevant in speech communication. Moreover, it is invaluable in terms of current requirements on the applications of linguistics, for instance in the speech synthesis of socially or regionally defined variants or in the field of forensic phonetics.

The sociophonetic function is also labelled as INDEXICAL. Prosody provides indices that characterize an individual; in other words, by using specific prosodic patterns we index various aspects of our social identity. Since people are social beings, their membership in various groups provides an essential set of descriptors. The term indexical, however, covers one additional aspect: that of idiosyncrasies in speech. There are specific features, or rather combinations of features that are particular only to a given speaker. They can be used to identify just him or her.

At various periods of history, the AESTHETIC FUNCTION was either emphasized or disregarded. Highly organized and ornamented texts were sometimes suggested to provide a model according to which other texts should be judged. The opposite extreme is typical of our times: artistic texts are argued to have little relevance since they are too rare. Both extreme stances are obviously wrong. Texts in which their authors aspire at aesthetic impact have their important place in language use; we maintain that they are neither irrelevant, nor do they serve as models for texts which are created for other purposes. They should be studied with regard to the values they provide to their recipients. It has to be emphasized that there is no binarity in the manifestation of the aesthetic function. A degree of elegance or refinement can be found in many texts of non-artistic nature. Even short conversational narratives (i.e., accounts of various events) can be evaluated in terms of the 'beauty' of their delivery. People can experience aesthetic sensations whenever language is used – the difference is just in the probability of their occurrence. As there is a large variation in people's sensitivity to aesthetic features, substantial opportunities for research, specifically for perception experiments, are open in this respect.

Finally, the LEXICAL FUNCTION of prosody is theoretically controversial. If prosody is defined as supralexical modulation of the sound of utterances, then there is no place for it. If, however, we admit that prosodic phenomena (see below) can be used to form proper shapes of lexical items, then lexical function can be discussed. It is very obvious in the so-called TONE LANGUAGES, in which melodic features participate in the design of individual words. To restate this from the point of view of a native Czech speaker, a word in tone languages is not just a string of phones – it is properly formed only when a string of phones is accompanied with a correct melodic feature. Identical strings of phones with different melodic characteristics are different words. Even non-tone languages may have traces of the lexical function. Swedish, for instance, has several hundred word pairs whose form differs only in the accent applied. Similarly, there are word pairs in English that differ only in the stress placement (e.g., *insult* as a noun and as a verb). Whether the lexical function belongs to prosody or not is left to the reader to decide.

As already noted, individual functions can hardly be expected to operate on their own. In speech communication, they combine and complement each other, which may complicate their description. It is, therefore, useful to realize that categorization of functions is by nature heuristic. It was suggested at various historical moments and since it proved useful, it was accepted. Nevertheless, it is a product of human minds and not necessarily the best (or even 'true') model of reality.

The preceding paragraphs could be concluded by introducing several terms that organize their contents. First of all, prosody manifests through PROSODIC PHENOMENA: melody, rhythm, tempo, timbre contrasts and distribution of loudness. Within those, more specific, locally distinctive PROSODIC EVENTS can be identified: prominence, boundary (or break), and configuration (or pattern). Analytically, the phenomena or events can be discussed in terms of PROSODIC DOMAINS that correspond with acoustic descriptive dimensions: the melodic domain relates to fundamental frequency, the temporal domain relates to duration, the domain of loudness is linked with soundwave amplitudes, and timber contrasts correlate with spectral features. If these domains appear in an experimental design, they can be relabelled as PROSODIC FACTORS (possibly also as PERCEPTUAL CUES). Let us conclude this paragraph with a reminder that we relate PROSODIC FUNCTIONS to the communication of meanings.

In addition, one more terminological note is necessary. Language is an abstract system whose properties can be observed only in the specific instances of its use: the texts. Based on their experience, schoolchildren sometimes believe that texts are only written. They hear, for instance: *Read out this text* or *Excerpt the text in your reader*, while instructions like *Listen to my explanatory text* are not customary. However, functional linguistics finds it quite useful to employ the term *text* for both spoken and written instantiation of language (Halliday & Matthiessen, 2014: 3). That is how we will refer to (spoken) texts also in this monograph.

1.3 DESCRIPTION OF SPEECH PROSODY

There are various approaches to describing speech prosody. One of the sources of this disarray must be the independence of various attempts in different locations of the world and different times in human history. Nowadays, however, sharing information across the globe is relatively easy, and records of historical achievements are available without much difficulty. Still, a united framework of prosody description is nowhere near.

The second cause of disunity is the dissatisfaction of individual scholars with the traditions they were brought up with. This leads to attempts at new descriptive frameworks. As long as such attempts are honest (not motivated by ambition to come with something striking at any price), they are praiseworthy. In fact, they are more than that: in all scientific fields, they are essential for any progress to be made.

However, there are some persistent points of confusion in prosody research that should be dealt with. Hardly anyone would disagree with the fact that prosody rests on four acoustic dimensions: FREQUENCY, DURATION, AMPLITUDE and SPECTRUM. (An objection by a theoretician that spectrum already combines frequencies and amplitudes is valid in certain niches of acoustics but not in general phonetics. This is because phonetics is obliged to take human perception as pivotal.) These objectively measurable acoustic dimensions are sometimes confused with the prosodic domains or factors (see above) that build on them. This can be misleading since human perception is geared to make use of acoustics in communication, but not to measure it objectively. Thus, phenomena like MELODY, TEMPO, LOUDNESS and TIMBRE are based on FREQUENCY, DURATION, AMPLITUDE and SPECTRUM, respectively, but they are not the same thing. (In the context of prosody research, the term frequency usually means fundamental frequency, f_0, unless stated otherwise.)

Another thing that has to be accented at the outset is that although each of these four domains can be described on its own (and this is very often the case due to the immense complexity of speech structure), they always function together as an aggregate. They influence each other considerably and there are currently no complete models of their mutual interactions. For instance, contours of f_0 are taken as the foundation of melodic movements in speech, yet experiments show that if a speaker slows down on a syllable or pronounces it louder, the otherwise identical course of f_0 will be perceived as a different melody. This applies the other way round as well: melody will influence the percept of tempo and loudness. That is why, unfortunately, there is no method of direct transformation of acoustic measurements into perceptual schemes.

Apart from differences, there are also similarities, at least in general approaches to the description of prosody (also called 'prosody modelling' nowadays). It can be noted that four main topics (aspects) are regularly present:
(1) building elements,
(2) prosodic syntax,
(3) operational space,
(4) factorial trends within utterances.

Let us discuss them individually. Since the description of the melodic domain is the most advanced (due to the apparent salience of melodies), we will mostly use examples from it. As the research in prosody progresses, we can expect analogous occurrences in other domains as well.

The BUILDING ELEMENTS are supposed to be the central constituents of the wholes. Such a whole may be an utterance or a prosodic phrase (see Chapter 2). The two most commonly used elements in current descriptions are either CONFIGURATIONS, or LEVELS. Briefly speaking, configurations are melodic falls, rises, fall-rises, etc. Levels are pitch targets that speakers aim at. The proponents of the level approaches claim that configurations are only by-products of target realizations. There have been various numbers of levels suggested as necessary for melody modelling. For Czech intonology, four levels were proposed by Daneš (1957), while the current internationally prevailing system ToBI uses only two (Beckman & Ayers, 1997). This two-level system was originally put forward for standard American English (Pierrehumbert, 1980), but was adopted for many other languages as well. The two levels used are H (for high) and L (for low). The system uses various rules to handle targets that were placed on different heights in earlier multilevel frameworks.

Most of the Czech tradition in melody description is configurational, though. It is generally focused on the configurations in phrase-final stress-groups, which are considered the most important characteristic for the correct interpretation of the meaning (especially in simple one-phrase utterances that are often used both in explanations and in research). The phrase-final stress-groups are said to host the MELODEME: a melodic scheme defined by its function. Melodemes are represented by various cadences defined by their shapes. For example, a conclusive falling melodeme may be implemented by a rising-falling cadence in Czech.

We respect the tradition in Czech intonation research, but still consider the term melodeme not entirely suitable for more comprehensive modelling. As stated in the fourth paragraph of this section, the prosodic domains are always aggregated, and they influence each other. Just because melody is the most conspicuous for conscious analytical observation, we do not find it practical to put other cues aside. It has been observed informally that identical melodies with different temporal properties are interpreted differently. The same effect can be observed if the loudness is distributed differently, or the voice quality is altered. Therefore, the term PROSODEME would be better motivated from the current point of view. However, if a researcher wants to declare an abstract approach and focus on melody solely, the term melodeme may be adequate.

In the British tradition, which is also configurational, the melodemes are called *tones* (e.g., O'Connor & Arnold, 1973; Wells, 2006; Roach, 2009). In the level approach, the melodeme or tone has to be described as a sequence of highs (H) and lows (L) specified as a nuclear pitch accent (with a * sign) together with a phrase accent (with a - sign) and a boundary tone (with a % sign). An example of such a symbolic string could be H* L- L%, which would stand for an unmarked cadence of the concluding falling melodeme.

As mentioned above, the concept of melodeme is defined by its function, while that of cadence or pitch accent by its form. For the sake of illustration, let us consider the continuation melodeme in Czech. This melodeme fulfils important roles with respect to all three basic components of meaning. In the representational component, it shows which words belong together and which should be perceived as belonging to another semantic grouping of words. In the conative component, the continuation melodeme invites the listener to keep listening and refrain from talking. In the affective component, the melodeme has the capacity to signal the importance of the unit in which it resides. The Czech continuation melodeme is represented by a rich variety of cadences (Volín, 2008a) that can be translated into the level-based description (Duběda, 2011).

A criterion orthogonal to the previous one divides descriptions of prosody to HIERARCHICAL and LINEAR ones. The hierarchical approach is also known as SUPERPOSITIONAL. It resonates with the traditional view of language as a hierarchical system: larger units can be dismantled into smaller unit. The hierarchy of prosodic units is presented in Chapter 2. The famous Fujisaki computational model of Japanese intonation (or rather f_0 tracks) had only two layers: phrasal and accentual (Fujisaki, 1983), while the above-mentioned hierarchy by Nespor and Vogel contains seven layers (Nespor & Vogel, 1983: 123). The superpositional approach inspired Dwight Bolinger to come up with the metaphor of "ripples on waves on swells on tides" (Bolinger, 1964: 282).

The proponents of linear modelling, on the other hand, claim that the hierarchy is only a visible consequence of a certain analytical approach. According to them, both speakers and listeners code and decode their messages only linearly, i.e., step by step in one layer. At any moment in an utterance, they allegedly know the next possible step given the preceding one without referring to any layers. The resulting hierarchy has no place in their neurolinguistic processing (see, e.g., Ladd, 2000).

One less common approach should still be mentioned here, at the end of the discussion concerning the building elements of prosody. If a scholar decides that the wholes are texts and the elements are prosodic phrases (or WORD GROUPS as in O'Connor & Arnold, 1973), he or she is said to be taking a HOLISTIC APPROACH. In such a case, what we describe above as elements are only auxiliary items of description. The holistic approach is a tempting but highly challenging strategy, since it leads either to large numbers of patterns or to massive simplifications (e.g., Armstrong & Ward, 1926). In the melodic domain, the holistic approach takes utterance TUNES as the wholes (see, e.g., O'Connor, 1980).

The second aspect of prosody description in our list is PROSODIC SYNTAX. Once an inventory of building elements is prepared, it is necessary to examine how these elements combine, in which positions they can occur, and what are the constraints on their occurrence. Prosodic-syntactic descriptions are also concerned with models of typical syntactic wholes, examples of 'marked' constructions, etc. An example of a prosodic-syntactic rule from Czech is the phrase-final position of the melodeme (prosodeme): in unmarked phrases, the melodeme starts on the last stressable syllable. An example of a typical construction in British intonology is the following sequence of parts: prehead + head + tonic syllable + tail. In this general scheme, possible candidates for individual positions are specified, and constraints on certain combinations are listed.

An interesting topic in research is also the correspondence between prosodic syntax and grammatical syntax. There are studies that quantify the co-occurrence of prosodic boundaries with syntactic divisions (see Section 2.3). Certain typical co-occurrences may be captured by orthographic rules, specifically by rules of comma insertion. For instance, dependent clauses in Czech have to be separated from the main clause by a comma. Such rules have to be relatively simple and unambiguous so that spellers are successfully guided towards 'correct' performance. However, the rules of prosodic syntax are probabilistic and also take account of the length of the constituents or the contextual need of emphasis, so the spelt comma does not have to be reflected in speaking, and no 'mistake' is necessarily made in such cases. The opposite is also possible. To place a comma between the subject and predicate of a sentence is banned. Nonetheless, a prosodic break is regularly present in this position (*cf.* Volín, Řezáčková & Matoušek, 2021). Remarkably, Miroslav Grepl reports that in medieval scripts and even in the early era of the Enlightenment, a rule existed for writing a comma between the subject and predicate if they were extended (Grepl & Karlík, 1986: 22). We investigated the issue of prosodic boundary between these two main syntactic constituents in our corpus of spoken Czech, and the results are presented in Section 4.3.

The third descriptive aspect is that of the OPERATIONAL SPACE. Each prosodic factor operates within certain limits that determine its range of values or SPAN. Apart from this range, it is useful to relate the space to some kind of referential point, thus establishing its LEVEL. If we decide to work with three possible spans (compressed, normal, expanded) and three levels (low, normal, high), we get nine combinations that can be tested or sought in various communicative situations and under various conditions. The fact that the perception of the two dimensions of the operational space (i.e., span and level) might be continuous and categories are invoked only for metalinguistic purposes does not invalidate experimenting. Little is currently known about the perceptual impact of various settings of operational space, but their importance is generally accepted.

It is customary to express the limits of the space by the acoustic minimum and maximum. In descriptive statistics, the distance between this lowest and highest value is called variation range (which somehow corresponds to what we labelled span in the preceding paragraph). However, Patterson and Ladd (1999) suggested that human perception of span does not correlate with the distance between maximum and minimum, but rather with the distance between the 10th and 90th percentile of the values. It is as if humans ignored the very extremes since those are often accidental outliers.

The level of the operational space is often quantified as the median or arithmetic mean. For specific research tasks, these values need to be normalized to allow for cross-speaker comparisons. Even then, though, this current practice is detached from the perceptual point of view that is essential for language users. Clearly, further work is required in the field of perceptual phonetics.

Two more cautionary notes still need to be put forward. First, the operational space in the melodic domain is often called the pitch range in current literature. Readers have to find out in each particular case whether the author actually means just span (as the term would suggest), or the construct with two dimensions (level and span) as advocated, for instance, by the above-cited Patterson and Ladd (1999). Second, the operational space can differ for various language varieties, communicative genres, groups of speakers, or even individuals. Furthermore, the operational space is typically used to signal certain attributes of affective states. For instance, span seems to correlate with the affective arousal axis (e.g., Banse & Scherer, 1996). This opens a large area of research topics.

The last aspect on our list and, at the same time, probably the last to be historically accepted into prosody description (*cf.* Volín & Šturm, 2021), is that of FACTORIAL TRENDS in utterances. The four chief factors listed in Section 1.2 (pitch, tempo, loudness, and timbre) may display certain global drift in one or the other direction within various speech stretches (see, e.g., Fig. 4.17). Such a speech stretch is typically a prosodic phrase or utterance, but trends in paragraphs have also been observed (e.g., Sluijter & Terken, 1993).

The existence of such trends was first noticed in the melodic domain for the factor of pitch. That explains why the trends were most extensively described just there (e.g., Pike, 1945; Cohen, Collier & t'Hart, 1982; Ladd, 1983, 1988; Gussenhoven & Rietveld, 1988; Gårding, 1998; Volín, 2008b). It was established that although in individual cases the trend can be in any direction, the downward tendency in the melodic domain is prevalent. Originally, this downtrend was attributed to mere physiology, but it was later discovered that this phenomenon is independent of the volume of air in the lungs. In many languages, downtrends can serve phonological function: phonologically identical events (usually pitch accents) in utterances can be downstepped or not, with downstepping usually considered unmarked. Nowadays, the term DECLINATION is used for an automatic, gradual drift to lower values, whereas DOWNSTEP is used for local lowering of a pitch target with phonological validity. Eventually, FINAL LOWER-ING was also added as a specific type of downtrend. It refers to an enhanced excursion from an otherwise monotonous (linear or exponential) trendline in the final portion of a speech unit (e.g., Liberman & Pierrehumbert, 1984; Palková et al., 2004).

A downtrend or uptrend might occur in other domains as well, but the research there is not as abundant as in the melodic one. In the temporal domain, final deceleration (often referred to as final lengthening) is well attested and is comparable to the above-mentioned final lowering. However, the tendency to a gradual temporal trend throughout a speech unit is not often investigated (but *cf.* Volín & Skarnitzl, 2007). It can be hypothesized that the slower tempo in the later part of an utterance may reflect its information structure. New information is delivered at a slower rate, whereas the given (contextually established) referents are articulated faster (e.g., Hapka, 2023).

A terminological note here seems necessary. The speaker can use various tempi to emphasize or de-emphasize certain words or word groups (see also parenthetical forms under the grammatical function of prosody in Section 1.2). This faster and slower production of linguistic units can be translated into their shorter and longer durations. Mathematically, this is undoubtedly correct. In phonetics, however, our ultimate concern is the language user. Does it make sense to claim that the listener internally measures durations of words? We are convinced that it is more plausible to expect the perception of changes in tempo, which is also more compatible with the large body of research on speech and articulation rate. In light of this, the term final lengthening seems less suitable than FINAL DECELERATION. Moreover, the term lengthening is already established in the phonology of Czech (and of other languages) to denote derivational processes by which a short vocalic phoneme is replaced by a long one (for example, *ustoupit* ['ustoupɪt] as a verb meaning *to retreat* has a related noun *ústup* ['uːstup], or *vyletět* ['vɪlecet] as a verb meaning *to fly out* has a related noun *výlet* ['viːlet] meaning *a trip*). This phoneme substitution cannot be interpreted as some sort of durational expansion of the same phoneme. (Importantly, Czech lexical stress does not manifest through longer durations of stressed vowels.)

Finally, as with previous aspects of description, the factorial trends can differ across language varieties, communicative genres, etc. (see, e.g., Umeda, 1982). Therefore, our own investigations included this fourth aspect of description as one of the key components of the analyses presented in Section 4.2.

2. PROSODIC UNITS

Language is considered a system of systems harbouring, among other things, the principle of hierarchical organization. Indeed, various compositional hierarchies (or rank scales) can be identified in individual domains of linguistic inquiry (e.g., Halliday & Matthiessen, 2014: 21). Given the immense diversity in the sound patterns of the world's languages, there is not a single hierarchy completely suitable for some sort of universal description. Unfortunately, due to historical isolation of various centres of phonetic research, there is not much unity in terminology either. Thus, even one carefully edited monograph can host several sets of terms for more or less identical units. Hirst and Di Cristo, for instance, provide an example of five different three-level prosodic hierarchies used by authors in their volume (Hirst & Di Cristo, 1998: 36).

The hierarchical view of language can consider larger units as either assembled from smaller units, or analysable into smaller units. Although both options sound the same, there is a fundamental difference. Traditional descriptions introduce the smallest units first and proceed to larger and larger text constituents. This approach is didactically justifiable, since the small units are simpler to describe and come in more limited inventories. However, there is an unfortunate side effect: students are led to believe that we plan our speech production phoneme by phoneme, and when listening to someone, we assemble the message from individual phonemes. There is a large body of research on formulaic language (and not only on that) that contradicts this simplistic and neurophysiologically very uneconomical concept (e.g., van Lancker & Canter, 1981; Wray, 2002; Ellis, 2003; Lin, 2018).

In our brief overview that follows, we will therefore proceed from larger units to smaller ones with the exception of the utterance. We start with it since we consider it the principal unit in the functional approach to language.

2.1 UTTERANCE

It must be emphasized right at the beginning that we consider an UTTERANCE the central unit of any comprehensive semantic analysis. The main reason is that it comprises a momentary 'logical whole', i.e., a communicative action (or reaction) that is under given circumstances in a way complete. There are scholars who talk specifically about a 'complete idea' (*cf.* Trost, 1962). It does not matter whether this sort of completeness rests in a very simple, perhaps even a one-word utterance, or in a unit of great syntactic and semantic complexity.

An utterance can be conceived as an equivalent to a SENTENCE with an important difference between the two: a sentence is an abstract scheme resulting from and serving metalinguistic analysis, while an utterance is a concrete minimal spoken text used in specific historical and social contexts with a specific extralinguistic purpose. (As such, this concept of an utterance should not be confused with a general meaning of the uncountable noun UTTERANCE as something unrestricted that has been uttered.)

A degree of completeness is presumably the precondition (and perhaps also an inner impulse) for the speaker to produce this fundamental unit of language use. Utterances are felt by both their producers and their perceivers as semantically concluded, although they quite often invite further utterances to develop the existing state of affairs. They are produced with the aim to make a discrete step towards the communicative intention of the interlocutors in the given context.

Although the utterance structure can be analysed, and smaller meaningful units can be identified (e.g., syntactic constituents, words, morphemes, etc.), those smaller units should not be considered primary. Human mind searches for them only when we already know what situational/contextual semantics needs to be voiced. That is, we proceed from our momentary intentions to verbal acts. In a healthy individual, the function precedes the form.

An utterance is the elementary agency of affecting the world (even if it is only in the sense of the addressee's relationship to the world). Through influencing addressees, communicants (hope to) achieve their goals. This is a serious fact that gives linguistics its social relevance. Therefore, even if utterances are sometimes menacingly complex, linguists should be brave enough to accept that they are the primary units of language use.

The above-stated does not in any case mean that all linguists should abandon their objects of inquiry and turn to utterances. It only means that studying, for instance, morphological detail, phonological differences between languages, lexical collocations, acquisition of intonation by infants, etc., should always be done with the awareness of the fact that, in the end, it is the utterance that matters to language users.

Lay people may voice their conviction that words are primary. Indeed, their proper choice and placement makes utterances comprehensible, effective, even elegant, or, on the contrary, clumsy, even nonsensical or unintelligible. Yet, on their own, words are extremely ambiguous. Each word has a potential to stand for various meanings. Most language users do not realize this since only the appropriate context is at the forefront of their minds and competing meanings are unconsciously blocked. Yet, everyone can certainly testify that one-word utterances with poor contextual grounding are frustrating. The simple affirmative particle *ano* (yes) can easily mean *What do you want?* or *Are you sure about that?* or *Will you provide more information?* or *I am beginning with my version* or *Despite expectations, it worked* or *Look how he messed up!* All that is needed for these disparate meanings to be perceived is the proper context and proper prosody. If these are present, no one's brain digs for alternatives.

Therefore, it is possible to select the WORD as a primary constructional unit (even if morphologists might not agree), but the UTTERANCE is still the primary unit of language use since it is its meaning that language users aim at and that they strive to put forward in the communication process.

As hinted above, a detached scheme of an utterance is called the SENTENCE. This term is confusing outside linguistics since the general public does not differentiate between sentences and utterances. In everyday talk, people rarely see the difference between abstract structures and specific language use materialized in spoken texts. In lay discourse, the label sentence is habitually used for specific utterances. However, the need to differentiate between sentence and utterance has been seriously discussed for more than a century (for an overview and useful references see Nekvapil, 1987), and the results of these discussions favour the differentiation. The ensuing advantage is a better organized understanding of the language potentials and specific instances of language use (i.e., spoken or written texts) and a possibility to appreciate the conceptual contrast between the surface MEANING and the contextually conditioned SENSE (e.g., Hoskovec, 2010) that, again, linguistics should not shy away from.

Despite the lack of a perfect definition of either the sentence or the utterance, the terms have been successfully used, especially when discussing general linguistic problems. In the context of experiments with the so-called laboratory speech, the distinction can be cumbersome, since the defining property of an utterance is its social and historical contextual grounding. This property is even more important than the observed structural feature: typically, an utterance has a topic (explicit or implicit) and a comment on that. Although laboratory sentences usually comprise topics and comments, they are often isolated, i.e., semantically uprooted. Their social and historical grounding is artificial or completely missing. Speakers who are instructed to materialize such sentences automatically invent their own imaginary contexts. This is because our whole existence is intertwined with contexts and because we are so used to them that we do not develop a capacity to detach our thought from them. Conscious analytical thinking can focus on aspects seemingly without a context, but that is only an illusion caused by the limitations of our consciousness.

Given the immense variability in utterance structure, it is often emphasized that utterances can be too long to be held in active consciousness. Even though the utterance is the primary semantic unit, neurophysiological limitations of human brains require processing units that are easier to manage. Those typically comprise strings of four to five words (e.g., Chafe, 2001: 675) and are beneficial both to the speaker, who can plan and produce them 'in one piece', and to the listener, who can process them as a coherent unit. We introduce them in Section 2.3.

2.2 PHONOPARAGRAPH AND TURN

Utterances can be grouped by a hypertopic, i.e., there may be a few utterances developing one strand of thought or referring to the same object, person, or phenomenon. In writing, they would form a paragraph. School curricula often prescribe training in paragraph construction. Students are supposed to acquire the skill to recognize core ideas of their prospective texts, think of them as hypertopics and develop them into paragraphs. In natural conversations, it can be demonstrated that hypertopics also span a number of utterances. People seldom abandon a topic after just one remark.

In the past, some linguistic approaches based on lexical semiotics refused to acknowledge any phonological organization above the sentence. However, notions of higher-level structures can be found already in Trim (1959). Still quite a long time ago, Lehiste (1975) experimented with short PHONOPARAGRAPHS to see whether the same sentence would have identical intonational features if it occurred at the beginning, the end, or within the paragraph. She chose three sentences that could be permuted relatively freely and formed six possible orderings. An experienced speaker was asked to read out the 'paragraphs' from randomly shuffled printed cards with isolated sentences mixed into the set as well. Subsequent measurements confirmed differences among intonational features depending on whether an identical sentence occurred in one of the three positions in a paragraph or whether it was uttered in isolation. Just as words receive unequal prosodic status in utterances, individual utterances receive specific prosodic features in a phonoparagraph.

One of the pioneering works on discourse analysis (Brown & Yule, 1983) also discusses organization of sound units at the paragraph level. The authors use the term PARATONE rather than phonoparagraph and speak about special 'phonological prominence' at the beginning of the unit and various prosodic devices at its end. However, Wichmann (2000) warns that in her material any 'neat' arrangement was often obscured by the more pressing need to signal the INFORMATION STRUCTURE of individual utterances. By this, she means the degree of givenness of lexical elements and the contextually justified focus on some of them. Generally, if the speaker needs to emphasize a word to signal its importance or deaccent another to signal its contextual givenness, he or she may give up on marking the phonoparagraph structure. Although Wichmann does not reject the existence of prosodic constituency of this high level, she cautions against naïve expectations of clear and transparent markers like those on lower levels of prosodic structure. Systematic prosodic marking at the phonoparagraph level may thus be expected, for instance, in well-prepared talks delivered by skilful lecturers or in experienced narrators.

Unprepared monologues or spontaneous conversations are believed to display less orderly semantic organization. However, Chafe summarizes his research experience in claiming that adherence to certain formation rules is clearly observable even in the domain of spoken, unedited texts (e.g., Chafe, 2001). The whole field of conversation analysis is actually founded on that tenet (e.g., Sacks, Schegloff & Jefferson, 1974; Local & Walker, 2005; ten Have, 2007; Ogden, 2012), and conversation is even argued to be 'the prototypical use of spoken language' (Chafe, 1992: 19). Rather than in paragraphs, talk in interaction is organized in TURNS. Like paragraphs, these can comprise more than one utterance, but their affiliation to hypertopics is less well defined than in the case of paragraphs. A large body of research focused on turn beginnings and turn ends from various points of view, and multiple lexical, syntactic, gestural, and other markers have been identified. It is especially Ogden's work that unravels phonetic systematics of turn-taking (e.g., Ogden, 2001; Ogden, 2010; Zellers & Ogden, 2013; Ogden, 2023). Interestingly, it is also Ogden who warns against separating segmental aspects from prosody too strictly, pointing out that interactional functions are fulfilled jointly by segments and suprasegments.

2.3 PROSODIC PHRASE

Utterances present relatively complete reactions to internal or external inducements to a speaker (see Section 2.1 above). Their structure varies immensely due to multiple requirements of the speaking style, communicative genre, context, or the specific needs and habits of the speaker. If an utterance is too long and/or too complex, it needs to be divided into smaller units that facilitate its processing in the addressee's brain.

These units have received disparate names due to various conceptual aspects and, also, historical chance. Older studies of rhetoric and versology used the term COLON, which is of Greek origin. Colon was roughly defined as a clause or part of a sentence that was prosodically separated from other parts. However, current consensus discourages the use of poetic terminology in phonetics, although the analogies should be appreciated; it is undoubtedly useful to understand how poetry uses the language potentials to produce its artistic qualities. On the other hand, the goals of poetry are too specific and too distant from communicative objectives in ordinary, thus, more frequent situations. Therefore, it would be quite awkward to make poetic norms, with their bias towards the aesthetic function, some sort of measure of general language use. Hence, relatively independent phonetic terms are seen as more suitable tools of analysis and description.

Czech phonetics has traditionally used the label PROMLUVOVÝ ÚSEK (UTTERANCE PART, or UTTERANCE SEGMENT; Palková, 1994). Although it sounds quite elegant and theoretically unobliging, the international literature written in English contains many other terms. For instance, Trager and Smith (1951: 50) proposed the term PHONEMIC CLAUSE for their highly abstract framework. Lieberman motivated his term physiologically when he suggested the term BREATH-GROUP as the key concept of his doctoral thesis (Lieberman, 1967: 2). One of his aims was to show how evolution could contribute to our understanding of the sound structure of languages. Interestingly, Lieberman's breath-group was not strictly physiological, so it did not require actual presence of inhaling as its delimitation. The reference to breath was used to underscore the phylogenetic foundation of speech properties.

Halliday's functional approach was phonetically more focused and led to the term TONE GROUP (Halliday, 1967), owing to the British intonological tradition that influenced his training. The tone within this framework refers to what is currently better known as NUCLEAR PITCH CONFIGURATION (or MELODEME in Czech). Interestingly, Halliday also introduces the term INFORMATION UNIT, which refers to an identical stretch of speech but focuses on different aspect of analysis (Halliday & Matthiessen, 2014: 215).

A widely used term nowadays is that of INTONATIONAL PHRASE (Nespor & Vogel, 1983; Ladd, 1986; Beckman, 1996), with its occasional variant INTONATION PHRASE (Pierrehumbert, 1980; Beckman & Ayers, 1997; Jankowski, Astésano & Di Cristo, 1999). Together with Chafe's INTONATION UNIT (Chafe, 1987, 1988) these latter terms emphasize the melodic dimension, which seems to suggest that various tunes are all that matters in phrasing. There are two possible explanations of this state. First, melodic cues are more salient to conscious observation than cues from other domains. Second, the term intonation in older conceptualizations covered not only the melody of speech (intonation in the narrow sense), but also loudness, tempo, and timbre (Roach, 1991). We believe, however, that with the increased awareness of the interplay of various perceptual cues of all auditory domains, it is more appropriate to use the term PROSODIC PHRASE. This view is also supported by the stabilization of the concept of prosody in the phonetic community in the last two decades. (The foundation of the Speech Prosody conference series in 2002 could be considered a moment that reflects the change.)

Interestingly, the cognitive importance of the prosodic phrase was already indicated about 80 years ago. The founder of the Prague Linguistic Circle, Vilém Mathesius, wrote:

> In typical pronunciation, the stream of speech is divided into meaningful units separated by pauses and united under one chief prominence. The more apparent this division is and the more responsive it is to the communicated contents, the clearer the message is and the easier it is to perceive it instantaneously. ... If the units are too short, the sense is shattered and the insight is lost. If the units are too long, the attention is overwhelmed with more information than can be taken in and the sense is mixed into chaos.
>
> (translated from Czech – Mathesius, 1943: 139)

The idea resonated extensively in the growing prosody research of the second half of the 20th century. Its very influential voicing occurred in the cognitively oriented work of Wallace Chafe. To him, the prosodic phrase (which he calls intonation unit – see above) is 'the expression of a single focus of consciousness' (Chafe, 1987: 32 in Lin, 2018: 49). With regard to their form, prosodic phrases materialize as '…relatively brief spurts of vocalization …(that) exhibit a single coherent intonation contour' (Chafe, 1988: 1). Given the transcription devices that he recommends to be used, it is clear that Chafe used the term intonation in its wider sense, i.e., comprising all prosodic dimensions.

More importantly, though, Chafe is concerned with the semantic contents of prosodic phrases. Using his corpus of spontaneous conversational speech, he illustrated his suggestion that the prosodic phrase is '…a linguistic expression of the particular information on which a speaker is focusing his or her consciousness at a particular moment' (Chafe, 1988: 2). According to him, division into prosodic phrases can be conceived as a reflection of the cognitive constraints on information quantity that human brains can process at a time. In other words, the prosodic phrase is a candidate processing unit that on some level serves to recover the intended meaning of spoken messages.

One of the recent pieces of evidence for this was already mentioned in Section 1.1. LaCroix and her colleagues carried out experiments in which they compared sentence comprehension by typical language users and patients with left hemisphere stroke, i.e., patients with impaired speech capacity. The facilitating effect of proper prosodic phrasing on comprehending the communicated meanings was clearly observed in both groups of subjects, even if in a different manner (LaCroix et al., 2020).

Although competent speakers divide their speech into prosodic phrases quite effortlessly, when asked to mark prosodic boundaries in speech recordings, they struggle. Even highly trained transcribers do not achieve perfect match of their judgements. There are two points which may be offered to explain this problem. First, transcribing is a metalinguistic task that requires competences very different from the linguistic ones. Analyzing language consciously is not the same as using it in typical speech behaviour, where many unconscious and semi-conscious processes are involved. Second, there are many different ways in which a prosodic boundary may be realized in speech. A possible list of perceptual cues or signals could be as follows (*cf.* also Section 5.1):

- final melodic configuration (nuclear pitch accent with boundary targets, melodeme),
- declination reset at the beginning of the next phrase,
- phrase-final deceleration (also known as lengthening),
- voice quality change (breathiness, creakiness),
- increase of nasality,
- intensity decrease,
- anacrusis at the beginning of the next phrase,
- pause.

Individual cues will be dealt with in the following chapters. Here, we will make just a brief note on the last item in the list, which seems trivial yet leads occasionally to confusion. The term PAUSE in this text means cessation of articulatory movements connected with construction of lexical units. Unlike some earlier researchers, we do not use the term for the prosodic boundary itself (*cf.* Petřík, 1938). It is well known that a PP boundary can be signalled by the presence of a pause, but a pause is neither a precondition nor unambiguous proof of a prosodic boundary. Yoon et al. (2007) worked with read-out speech of radio programmes (Boston University Radio Speech Corpus). A pause was present at a phrasal boundary about 40% of the time. More than one half of the phrasal boundaries occurred without pauses (Yoon at al., 2007: 1018).

A prosodic boundary can be made by combining any of the above. Moreover, the listed markers are not binary: their salience can be controlled gradiently by the speakers. It follows that no simple rules or deterministic detectors of prosodic boundaries exist. This fact leads back to the first point above. Whereas our metalinguistic knowledge is deterministic (in the form of various rules), our linguistic module (controlling the communicative use of the language) is probabilistic.

Despite this, many renowned researchers believe that the prosodic boundary continuum can be split into distinct categories. For prosodic phrases, two levels are usually proposed (e.g., Trim, 1959; O'Connor & Arnold, 1973: 4; Beckman & Pierrehumbert, 1986; Ladd, 1986). Currently, the best-known terms for these two levels are part of the ToBI convention (Beckman & Ayers, 1997). They are INTONATION PHRASE for the complete, potentially stand-alone unit, and INTERMEDIATE PHRASE for the unit that cannot stand on its own without causing sensation of an abrupt break. Although we accept the basis of this division, when necessary, we shall use the term MAJOR PROSODIC PHRASE as opposed to MINOR PROSODIC PHRASE.

Definitions of intonation and intermediate (major and minor) phrase are sometimes circular in that the intonation phrase is described to have a 'boundary tone' while the intermediate one only a 'phrase accent', but then both these events are recognized by their presence at the end of an intonation or intermediate phrase, respectively.

A rule of thumb that seems to be quite useful as a guidance says that after a major prosodic phrase, there is a possibility of a silent pause without any disturbing perceptual effects. This means that if all the perception cues lead to a satisfactory completion of a major prosodic phrase, a silent pause (perhaps with a breath intake) can be made or imagined. A minor phrase (intermediate phrase in ToBI), on the other hand, does not have boundary signals salient enough, so that the insertion of a silent pause would sound somehow 'disfluent', because there is either insufficient phrase-final deceleration or the melodic movement is too shallow.

Transcribers can testify, however, that there is a certain overlap between satisfactory and unsatisfactory completion, which leads to some degree of disagreement in individual assessments. A procedure that is recommended for research rests in multiple assessments with subsequent negotiations over unclear cases. Nevertheless, although various structural properties of a prosodic phrase can be mentioned, the crucial aspect remains to be perceptual: the prosodic phrase is a unit that can be experimentally demonstrated through the behaviour of listeners (Palková, 1994: 163 and 290).

A question that is often articulated with greater or lesser explicitness is that of correspondences between syntactic and prosodic boundaries. Speculative approaches used to assert that prosody 'serves' syntax and that 'correct' prosodic boundaries coincide with syntactic boundaries. Prosodic phrasing was then expected to parallel clauses. Empirical research has shown, however, that correspondences between syntactic and prosodic boundaries are far from perfect. Cruttenden (1997: 69) reports only 40% of matching boundaries. Chafe originally found a 70% match (1988: 3), but later lowered the number to 60% (1994: 66) and specified his material as informal conversation.

(He, however, suggests that the actual ratio fluctuates across speakers and situations. According to him, this feature deserves attention.)

An important aspect of this issue is that mismatch between prosody and syntax is not necessarily perceived as 'incorrect'. Listeners obviously pay attention to semantics of the messages, and as long as the division into phrases is coherent with what they perceive as sensible, no correspondence with syntax is required. An idea of separate 'service' of prosody and syntax to semantics was suggested in the field of conversation analysis (Auer, 1996). According to the author, syntax and prosody join 'their capacities' if the situation does not require otherwise, but they should be perceived as independent of each other. This view is very far from the old tenet that a prosodic break within a syntactic constituent is an error.

2.4 ACCENT GROUP, STRESS GROUP, FOOT

There are three units which have been proposed to describe speech at the level corresponding approximately to a word. The units are closely related to lexical stress and may be said to differ in the level of abstraction. The most abstract is the FOOT, a unit used largely in the rhythmical description of poetry. Poetry distinguishes between a number of foot types, such as the disyllabic iamb and trochee (with the rhythmical sequence weaker- stronger, and stronger–weaker, respectively), or the trisyllabic dactyl (stronger–weaker–weaker), etc. These types of feet are illustrated in Figure 2.1 on examples from Czech poetry (see Greene, Cushman, Cavanagh et al., 2012 for more on the rhythmical description of poetry and Kolár, Plecháč & Říha, 2013 specifically about Czech).

Abercrombie (1964; cited in Gibbon, 2015) used the term foot to describe the so-called left-headed rhythmic units beginning with a stressed syllable and containing optional unstressed syllables which follow the stressed one; this corresponds to the trochee and dactyl types mentioned above. A more sophisticated model of prosodic structure was proposed by Jassem (1952; cited in Gibbon, 2015); his model incorporates both rhythmical and tonal structure by including anacrusis as a sequence of proclitic

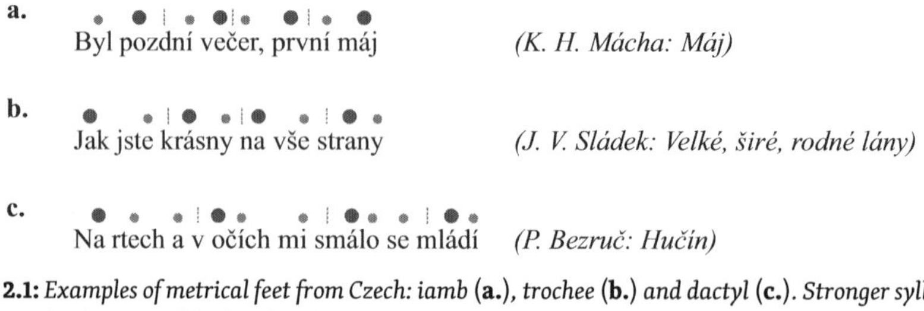

a. Byl pozdní večer, první máj (K. H. Mácha: Máj)

b. Jak jste krásny na vše strany (J. V. Sládek: Velké, širé, rodné lány)

c. Na rtech a v očích mi smálo se mládí (P. Bezruč: Hučín)

Figure 2.1: *Examples of metrical feet from Czech: iamb* (**a.**), *trochee* (**b.**) *and dactyl* (**c.**). *Stronger syllables are indicated in larger and darker dots than the weaker syllables; individual feet are divided by dashed vertical lines.*

unstressed syllables, the tonal group (which is equivalent to Abercrombie's foot) and prosodic juncture.

The units STRESS GROUP and ACCENT GROUP are defined as the stretch of speech from one stressed syllable to the next, but not including the next one. The distinction between them is analogical to that between the frequently used terms STRESS and ACCENT (Beckman, 1986): stress is often conceptualized as an abstract potential of a given syllable to carry prominence, while accent is understood as a prominence which has actually been realized (note, however, different approaches to these terms, for example in Sluijter & van Heuven, 1996). In a similar vein, then, a STRESS GROUP would also be considered a hypothetical unit, an abstraction based on the prototypical behaviour of words in a specific language, while ACCENT GROUP would correspond to actual groups of syllables joined into one prosodic unit by using specific surface manifestations of prominence (Volín & Skarnitzl, 2020). For instance, the word *groups* has a stress potential: /ˈgruːps/, but it is quite possible that this potential would not be realized and the word would not be accented in the sentence just above: [ˈæktʃuəlgruːps̬ əv ˈsɪləb̬lz]. This example shows that the clustering into accent groups will depend on a number of factors; apart from semantic and contextual considerations, these may include tendency to eurhythmy. That means that speakers tend to adjust the length of adjacent stress groups so as to produce speech with more regular rhythm (Giegerich, 1992: 273).

In many languages, an accent group is characterized by greater phonetic prominence of the accented syllable as opposed to the unaccented syllables. Acoustically, greater prominence may be achieved by a longer duration of the accented syllable, by (most typically) higher fundamental frequency (f_0) or a greater f_0 excursion, or by higher intensity or less steep spectral slope; from the perspective of the listener, an accented syllable would be perceived as longer, with a higher pitch or more salient melodic movement, and louder, respectively (Gordon & Roettger, 2017). In addition, relative prominence may be signalled by vowel quality, frequently manifested by the centralization of unaccented vowels towards the lax mid-central SCHWA. The extent to which these correlates of prominence are exploited is language-specific, partly to avoid multiple functions of a given cue: languages with contrastive vowel length like Czech or Finnish will therefore rely less on vowel duration, while tone languages like Vietnamese or Thai are less likely to make use of f_0 changes to signal prominence on the lexical level.

It also appears that prominence differences are more salient in languages in which lexical stress has a contrastive role (e.g., English or Spanish), whereas languages with stress fixed to a certain syllable within the word do not require strong prominence signalling (Cutler, 2005). Indeed, Czech – a language with stress on the first syllable of a stress group – has been shown to essentially lack any prominence signalling of the accented syllable: Skarnitzl (2018) reported that the vowel in the accented syllable tends to be slightly shorter than in the subsequent unaccented syllables, frequently has lower f_0 than the post-stressed syllable (see also Palková & Volín, 2003; Volín & Skarnitzl, 2022), its level in dB is virtually identical to that of unaccented syllables, and there are no clear differences in the quality of vowels in accented and unaccented syllables. It has thus been suggested that, rather than the prominence of a syllable, it is the configuration of acoustic qualities throughout the entire accent group, as well as their discontinuities at accent group boundaries, that marks lexical stress in Czech (Janota & Palková, 1974; Palková & Volín, 2003; Skarnitzl & Volín, 2019).

Returning to the joining of words into stress groups, many languages tend to avoid what is referred to as stress clash, that is, two consecutive stressed syllables. As a result, it is especially monosyllabic words that are likely to join the neighbouring word as enclitics and form a stress-group with it. For example, the English question *What will you do with it?* will probably be realized in two accent groups [ˈwɒtwɪljə ˈduːwɪðˌɪt]; similarly, the Czech sentence *To se mi moc nelíbí (I don't really like it)* will probably also comprise two accent groups [ˈtosɛmɪmo͡ts ˈneliːbiː]. Latest evidence (Volín & Skarnitzl, 2018; 2020) suggests that even words longer than the monosyllabic may function as enclitics in Czech. For instance, in the sentence *Zítra nebudu večeřet (Tomorrow I won't eat any dinner)* the second word, albeit three-syllabic, could easily remain unaccented [ˈziːtranɛbudu ˈvet͡ʃɛr̝ɛt]. However, more specific rules concerning the usage of longer enclitics in Czech have yet to be formulated.

2.5 SYLLABLE

Defining the SYLLABLE as a unit presents a challenging task. On the one hand, we have the syllable as a phonetic unit, presumably processed by the brain during speech articulation and perception. On the other hand, there is the syllable as a phonological unit, which describes the forms possible in a specific language system. Although different in kind, the two perspectives generally align in terms of the segments they encompass. However, discrepancies can arise, such as when a single phonological syllable corresponds to two phonetic syllables (or vice versa), or when certain segments are excluded from the phonological syllable (see Šturm & Bičan, 2021: 75–82, for examples and literature background).

Despite claims to the contrary (Kohler, 1966; Chomsky & Halle, 1968; Labrune, 2012), the syllable is currently considered important for describing the language system. Following Hyman (2011), we can identify at least four uses of the phonological syllable. Firstly, and perhaps most importantly, it serves as a domain for describing the distribution of phonemes. The syllable is 'a structural unit most economically expressing the combinatory latitudes of vowels and consonants within a given language' (O'Connor & Trim, 1953: 105). Secondly, it can aid in constraining the systematic variations in phonemes (capturing the distribution of some allophones) or in morphemes (capturing alternations). Thirdly, the syllable may condition the localization of some prosodic phenomena, such as stress, tone, or minimal word requirements. Finally, as we will see below, the syllable acts as a component of the prosodic hierarchy.

Regarding the phonetic syllable, various definitions have been proposed (e.g., Pike, 1947: 246; Stetson, 1951: 1; Laver, 1994: 114; Roach, 2009: 56; Browman & Goldstein,

1995: 20; Ménard, 2013: 270) but they share a common characteristic – the syllable is a unit of speech organization and coordination. Recently, Easterday defined the syllable as "a natural unit of spoken language by which sounds are organized in speech" (2019: 3). Importantly, the syllable is not only internally structured into segments but also organized within the broader domains of the prosodic hierarchy. Many scholars, including those in the Czech environment (Skaličková, 1954; Hála, 1956; Renský, 1960; Palková, 1994), emphasize its role as a carrier of prosodic features of speech, such as stress, intonation, and rhythm (which again allow for analyzing utterances into smaller units). Generally, the syllable is viewed as a more basic and more robust unit than the speech sound in both production and perception (Grossberg, 2003; Raphael, 2005; Kühnert & Nolan, 2006). Speech acquisition by children also manifests initial benefits for syllable representations over segmental representations (Jusczyk & Derrah, 1987; Eimas, 1999; Oller, 2000: 300–303; Hallé & Christia, 2012).

At least three positions are typically differentiated in a syllable. The NUCLEUS, which is usually a vowel but can sometimes be a consonant, is the essential element that defines the presence of a syllable. Any consonants preceding the nucleus form the ONSET of the syllable, while consonants following the nucleus form the syllable's CODA. For instance, in the word *brain*, /bɹ/ constitutes an onset cluster, /eɪ/ represents a nuclear vowel, and /n/ acts as a final coda. However, the syllabification of polysyllabic words, such as *function*, can be more intricate, requiring rules to determine the division of the medial sequence /ŋkʃ/ between syllables (for a comprehensive overview of syllabification procedures, refer to Šturm & Bičan, 2021: Chapters 4 and 5). The nucleus and coda are sometimes additionally merged into a RIME constituent (/eɪn/ in our example).

Languages exhibit considerable variation in the complexity of allowed syllable types (see, e.g., Blevins, 2006; Gordon, 2016; Easterday, 2019). While each language imposes specific restrictions on the composition and size of its onsets and codas, certain tendencies can be observed. Romance languages, for instance, have relatively simple syllable structures characterized by a limited range of syllable templates (e.g., V, CV, CVC, CCVC), with additional constraints on specific segments in each position. Spanish allows initial onsets such as /pl/ or /tr/ (*plato* 'dish', *truco* 'trick') where sonority rises towards the nucleus, while Czech permits similar sequences (*plavat* 'swim', *tráva* 'grass') as well as sequences with reversed sonority (*lpím* 'I dwell (on)', *rty* 'lips'). Moreover, Czech permits two obstruents in onsets (/st/, /gd/, /zʒ/), while Spanish does not. Codas also exhibit further limitations, with Czech displaying greater flexibility (allowing up to 3-4 consonants word-finally), while Spanish is limited to a single consonant in non-foreign words. In contrast, Germanic languages resemble Czech in terms of syllable complexity. German is well-known for its complex codas, exemplified by words like *Stumpf* or *Herbst*. English allows up to three consonants in the onset and up to four in the coda (e.g., *street* and *prompts*, respectively). However, the number of distinct syllables in English or German is considerably smaller than in Czech, indicating greater phonotactic restrictions on onsets and codas in these languages. It is worth noting that the simplicity of syllable structure in languages like Spanish, French and

Italian also has rhythmic implications, most notably in the different distribution of vocalic and consonantal intervals when compared to Germanic languages.

The possibilities in the languages of the world nevertheless encompass a broader range in both directions. A language can have only single-consonant onsets (Maori) while another may have even six consonants in the onset (Georgian). Easterday (2019) extended Maddieson's (2013) classification and identified four levels of syllable complexity: Simple, Moderately Complex, Complex, and Highly Complex. Czech belongs to the fourth type (Šturm & Bičan, 2021), defined as "languages in which the maximal onset or coda consists of three obstruents, or four or more Cs of any kind" (Easterday, 2009: 61). However, regardless of a language's maximal complexity, the occurrence of each syllable shape is highly skewed, with more complex syllables having substantially lower frequency within a language. This typically holds true for both onsets and codas.

The syllable bears significant importance in the exploration of prosodic structure and it is usually the smallest unit 'with a prosody'. There is a consensus regarding the foundational position of the syllable within the prosodic hierarchy, which is observed universally across languages. (It is worth noting that the MORA, characterizing syllables in terms of phonological weight, does not belong to a typical hierarchy; see Fox, 2000, p. 50 and 355).

3. ANALYZED MATERIAL

3.1 A GENERAL NOTE ON TERMS

Analyses presented in this monograph are for the most part based on speech material that represents three types of communicative situations, i.e., three genres; it is described in Sections 3.2 through 3.4. However, since there is considerable terminological confusion in phonetic sciences when it comes to speech style, speech genre or speech register, we will first explain how these terms are used in our book.

In line with the general understanding outside phonetics, we maintain that STYLES are defined by form, whereas GENRES by content. Although this statement sounds simple, there are some difficulties with its utilization. One of the main complications lies in the fact that certain contents require specific forms. A given style cannot be freely used in whichever genre without breaking cultural (i.e., social) norms. As a result, one of the terms is often used to cover both concepts. Commonly, the term genre is not used at all in phonetic discourse, while the term style is used with only a vague denotation. For instance, people talk about read and spontaneous speech referring to them as styles as if there was just one manner of reading out written texts, and one and only way to talk spontaneously in all situations. That, clearly, is not the case.

In our phonetic research practice, we find it useful to differentiate between speaking styles with reference to articulatory effort. Basically, greater effort results in higher clarity of the phonetic forms in speech and vice versa. (Articulation in a wider sense is meant here, so it could be more fitting to talk about speech production effort.) Table 3.1 presents the scale we use.

Many objections could be raised against this simplified scheme. First, we are dividing a continuum into categories, and therefore no clear boundaries between neighbouring styles can be defined. Second, articulatory (or speech production) effort cannot fully explain all the attributes of the resulting styles. The 'effort' is a metaphor that must not be taken literally, since it conceals important intentions of the speaker with regard to the listener (these are in a way present in the classification suggested by Joos, 1968). For instance, hyperarticulated or clear speech are supposed to be associated with moderate speech rates. Fast tempi would increase effort in both cases, but that is obviously not done because the effort would become ineffective (Lindblom, 1990). Third, even if perceptual considerations are included, there are still factors that con-

Table 3.1. *The classificatory scale of speaking styles.*

Style	Indicators
hyperarticulated	exaggerated articulatory gestures and enhanced contrasts in all phonological/perceptual domains
careful/clear	articulatory targets clearly reached, assimilatory processes limited, individual units of speech easily identifiable
ordinary	average effort with no salient deviation in any direction, no features attracting attention to the form
relaxed/casual	high degree of co-articulation, all standard assimilations and reductions together with occasional non-standard ones
hypoarticulated	highly suppressed contrasts, substantial number of elisions, indistinct segmental and prosodic forms

tribute to the resulting speech forms like preparedness and its correlate fluency (*cf.* also, e.g., Eskenazi, 1993). On the other hand, many research tasks can be accomplished just based on our simple scheme, so until more elaborate classifications are in common use, we will adhere to it.

Although GENRE is usually linked to suitable styles that are considered appropriate for it, it is defined by its communicative values. An important foundation of the concept of genre is the social context, the specific interactive purpose, and the set of hierarchically organized functions that the genre fulfils. All this influences the linguistic contents of the texts spoken in individual genres. Thus, a public political address belongs to a different genre than a university lecture, and a cooking show on television is not the same genre as a political debate on the same medium. There are many speaking genres that may be analyzed in hierarchical schemes, so unlike for styles, a complete *a-priori* classification can hardly be expected.

The term REGISTER is sometimes used to provide a combined perspective, overlapping to some extent with both genre and style (*cf.* Biber & Conrad, 2009: 2). Although we do not contradict the usefulness of such a concept, we will not use it in our book.

Having discussed the key terminological distinctions, we can now turn to the description of the speech material that serves as the foundation for all our analyses presented in the following chapter. As already mentioned in Chapter 1, we aimed at finding a compromise between, on the one hand, examining artificially designed texts recorded in a sound-treated laboratory with no communicative intent on the part of the speakers (other than to please the experimenter perhaps) and, on the other hand, recordings of spontaneous dialogues obtained in naturalistic conditions with all the incomplete sentences, overlaps, disfluencies and other phenomena, where the linguistic nature and phonetic manifestation of prosodic phrases might be quite opaque. Our compromise lies in analyzing three genres in which communicative intent was undoubtedly present, but which involve read speech obtained in high-quality conditions.

The texts in all these genres are well structured, and the speakers are supposed to use the style that is labelled as careful or clear in Table 3.1. The three genres are newsreading (also abbreviated as NWS), storytelling (STR), and poetry reciting (POR), and they will be described in more detail in the three sections that follow.

Our aim was also to be able to analyze speech material which is comparable across the three genres. For that reason, we will analyze sixteen speakers per genre (always eight females, eight males) and comparable amounts of speech per speaker, approximately three to five minutes (see below). All speakers are coded in an identical manner: in the code name, which contains three characters, the first character refers to the genre (P = poetry reciting, N = newsreading, S = storytelling), the second to the speaker's sex (F = female, M = male), and then a digit from 1 to 8 (thus, for example, NF2 = the second news reading female speaker, or PM4 = the fourth poetry reciting male speaker).

3.2 POETRY RECITING

Poetry reciting may be considered the strictest of the three genres in the sense that the rendition of a poem necessitates certain prosodic forms. In other words, there is much less 'leeway' for speakers to engage in idiosyncratic solutions in poetry reciting. Our 16 speakers were recruited from a large body of students and graduates of the Faculty of Arts, Charles University. They volunteered because of their express interest in poetry and in reading poetry; they received monetary reward for their participation. The recordings were obtained in the sound-treated studio of the Institute of Phonetics at the same institution, at a sampling rate of 32 kHz and with 16-bit quantization.

The speakers were instructed to read the poems quietly first so as to understand the sense, and then to practice them aloud. They were told to be mindful of the poems' rhythm but not to feel strictly bound by it. They were to imagine that they were delivering the poems for a future audience, that they had to engage the listeners, to transfer the spirit of the poems on to them. That is why each poem – with its preparation, practice, and recording – was treated as a separate unit; this enabled the speakers to portray the atmosphere and spirit of each poem, before turning to the next one.

From a larger set read by the speakers, we selected four poems from the 1910s and 1920s by three poets who belong to the group of anarchist rebels. One of the objectives of this selection was for the poems to differ slightly in how fixed their rhythmic structure was, in how much the speakers could 'play' with the realization. The total duration of the four poems was slightly below four minutes (230 seconds) on average and ranged between 195 seconds (speaker PM1) and 285 seconds (PM6).

Nevertheless, from the viewpoint of prosodic phrasing, the object of study in this book, the genre of poetry reciting (POR) was selected as one where prosodic structure was generally the most controlled.

3.3 NEWSREADING

The second subcorpus analyzed in this book consists of news bulletins read by 16 newsreaders of the Czech Radio. The recordings were obtained between 2004 and 2009; originally, they were recorded analogously from VHF broadcasting and subsequently digitized as WAV files at 22,050 Hz with 16-bit quantization.

Czech Radio is the nationwide public broadcaster in the Czech Republic, and its newsreaders may be regarded as bearers of standard pronunciation, as cultured and prestigious speakers. It is clear that their speech must be comprehensible, which should be reflected in their pronunciation at the segmental level, as well as in the realization of prosodic units. The occurrence of various speech mannerisms, which may be heard from newsreaders on commercial radio or television stations, should be restricted in public radio newsreaders.

One news bulletin on the Czech Radio typically comprises two signal calls (at the beginning, where the newsreaders welcome the audience, introduce themselves and announce the date, and at the end with a summary signal call) and several news items, most frequently between six and ten. These include domestic and foreign news, as well as sports news and the weather forecast. The duration of the individual news bulletins differs somewhat, depending on the number of newsworthy items and to some extent also on the time of day when the bulletin was broadcast; the mean duration of a bulletin is three and a half minutes (210 seconds), with the shortest news bulletin being 110 seconds (speaker NM1) and the longest one 276 seconds long (speaker NM2).

In terms of prosodic rendition of phrases, newsreading was expected to provide more variability than poetry reciting in the sense that newsreaders have more choice: they are likely to observe the semantic and pragmatic aspects of the news items, rather than the rhythmical requirements of the sentences. On the other hand, newsreaders may manifest some stereotypical speech behaviours, for example specific melodic movements. Most importantly, the semantic content of the individual news items – for instance whether the presented latest economic results are positive or negative, or whether the national sports team has won or lost – should not affect the prosodic realization on public radio. In this sense, we may see the prosody in newsreading (NWS) as semi-controlled.

3.4 STORYTELLING

The storytelling subcorpus consists of extracts from audiobooks, read by 16 professional Czech actors. We only selected audiobooks which were read by a single actor. The recordings were downloaded as high-quality MP3 files (typically with a data flow of 320 kbps) and converted to WAV files for easier analysis.

It is to be expected that the speaking behaviour of professional actors will be much more variable than in newsreading. Some of the passages in the audiobooks were of narrative character, some involved direct speech, some were emotionally charged. For example, the actors used variations in speech rate to reinforce the message which was to be conveyed much more. On the other hand, excessive variability was not desirable for our purposes, and care was thus taken to avoid passages (or, in fact, entire audiobooks) where the actor changed their voice considerably to portray different characters. Such audiobooks would be a fascinating object of study for a different purpose than the one we had in this monograph, for example the examination of the flexibility and plasticity of human voices.

Unlike in newsreading, it was easier to control the duration of the analyzed speech material: audiobooks typically contain hours of speech. This allowed us to extract a minimum of five minutes of speech per speaker; the mean duration was five and a half minutes (330 seconds), with 312 seconds being shortest (speaker SF6) and 360 seconds being longest; this longer duration was selected because speaker SM6 was reading at a considerably slower speech rate than the other actors.

In storytelling (STR), the prosodic rendition was dictated by a larger combination of factors, including the affective 'charge' of the specific sentences, the character portrayed in cases of direct speech, but also the speakers' possible idiosyncratic habits. Crucially, in contrast with poetry reciting and especially newsreading, the storytelling genre itself did not impose any global requirements on the speakers' performance. From this perspective, we regard storytelling as the least controlled of the three genres analyzed in this monograph.

3.5 PRE-PROCESSING

In order to be able to extract all the information about prosodic phrasing from the collected speech samples, it was necessary to turn them from raw recordings into an appropriately annotated corpus. That consisted of several stages. First, we used Prague Labeller, an HMM-based forced alignment tool (Pollák, Volín & Skarnitzl, 2007), to detect boundaries of individual speech sounds. In a painstakingly long process, those were then corrected manually using phonetically motivated guidelines (Machač & Skarnitzl, 2009).

When all boundaries of speech sounds (and by extension, of individual words) were correctly placed – that is, when processing at the segmental level was finished – it was possible to start analyzing the prosodic structure of the recordings. This involved the location and classification of prosodic phrase boundaries, and identification of stress group boundaries. If identifying segmental boundaries constitutes a challenge, annotating prosodic structure is even more complex. All prosodic cues – melody, loudness dynamics, temporal relations, and voice quality – may be involved in intricate combinations, making a syllable stressed at the stress group level, or final at the prosodic phrase level. It takes concentrated repeated listening, including narrower and broader context, to arrive at a decision. Prosodic annotation was therefore undertaken by two of the authors: one always checked the other's annotations, and any potential ambiguities or uncertainties were discussed during joint sessions and resolved. Throughout the corpus, one of the authors always checked 100% of the work of the other author. On average, discord or doubts occurred over 2-3% of the labels in a set. Such cases were reanalyzed together, and agreement was negotiated.

Prosodic boundary labelling was carried out following the ToBI conventions (Beckman & Ayers, 1997, but *cf.* also here Section 2.3 for terminological adjustment), in which five depths of boundaries are defined and assigned break indices (BIs). Whereas BIs 0, 1, and 2 are important for stress-group identification, phrasal boundaries are associated with the BI3 or BI4 definitions. Section 2.3 presents eight typical cues of phrasal boundaries. The two that are most easily accessible to conscious observation are phrase-final deceleration and a specific terminal melodic configuration. If we refer to just these two, we can briefly summarize that minor prosodic phrase (intermediate phrase in ToBI) ends with an aggregate that would not be perceptually satisfactory before a pause: either the melodic movement is not salient enough or the phrase-final deceleration is absent. (The latter was much more common in our material than the former.) These cases were labelled with BI3.

Major prosodic phrase (concluded with BI4), on the other hand, has a clear phrase-final deceleration and, at the same time, a well-shaped terminal melodic configuration. We observed, however, that in our material, there is something more than these two signals, so it is more accurate to talk about such a combination of cues following which a pause (real or potential) does not create unsatisfactory sensations. In other words, the label BI4 must refer to a satisfactory closure of a group of words, after which a pause (i.e., cessation of lexical item articulation) would be possible. Let us note, however, that this closure does not necessarily mean an end of an utterance. It plainly means a perceptually clear end of a prosodic phrase. Another phrase belonging to the same utterance may easily follow. Thus, utterance-final and utterance-internal phrases can display the same depth of division marked with BI4. This is an example of such a structure (produced by speaker SM1):

'Kromě 'toho | 'že bral 'příležitostně 'kokain ‖ 'neměl 'jiné 'neřesti ‖
(Besides the fact | that he occasionally took cocaine ‖ he had no other vices ‖)

It has to be explained that in our examples, breaks after major prosodic phrases (BI4) are transcribed with double vertical line: ‖, while breaks after minor phrases (BI3) are transcribed with a single vertical line: |.

4. PROSODIC PHRASE IN CONTEMPORARY CZECH

This chapter constitutes the analytical bulk of this monograph. It will provide three perspectives on prosodic phrasing in the genres described above. In Section 4.1, we examine the structure of prosodic phrases: their length, the distribution of minor (BI3-type) and major (BI4-type) phrases, as well as some more detailed analyses. Section 4.2 presents the results of acoustic analyses: we will be interested in the slope of acoustic prosodic parameters like fundamental frequency or intensity throughout prosodic phrases. The last section of this chapter focuses on syntactic characteristics of prosodic phrases, particularly the relationship between the subject and the predicate.

4.1 PROSODIC PHRASE STRUCTURALLY

Previous empirical findings (see Volín, 2019; Skarnitzl & Hledíková, 2022 for comparisons of Czech and English) as well as informal observations indicated that prosodic phrases in Czech are in some measures considerably longer than in other languages, but also that this may be, not surprisingly, to a certain extent, genre-specific. The goal of this section is therefore to present the first systematic investigation of the structure of the prosodic phrase in three genres of Czech. Apart from reporting global and individual tendencies concerning the length of phrases and stress groups in subsections 4.1.1 and 4.1.2, respectively, we will focus on two phenomena which have received little attention – and even less empirical attention – in Czech phonetic literature, namely anacrusis (subsection 4.1.3) and monosyllabic stress groups (subsection 4.1.4). The analyses are based on the manually coded properties of prosodic phrases and stress groups in Praat TextGrids.

For statistical comparisons, we constructed generalized linear mixed-effects (GLME) models in R (R Core Team, 2017) using the *lme4* package (Bates et al., 2015). The count of the respective unit served as the dependent variable. Fixed effects will be described with the first analysis in the next section; SPEAKER was always specified as random intercept. The significance of fixed effects was tested by comparing the full model to a model with the given factor excluded using likelihood ratio tests. Plots showing mean values of the measured variables and their confidence intervals were created using the *emmeans* package (Lenth, 2023) and visualized with *ggplot2* (Wickham, 2016).

4.1.1 PHRASE LENGTH

The length of prosodic phrases in the three subcorpora – storytelling (STR), newsreading (NWS) and poetry reciting (POR) – is shown in Figure 4.1, expressed in the number of stress groups, words, syllables, and phones. As is to be expected, all histograms are skewed to the right. Perhaps the most striking result is that if we calculate the modal value of all four units (that is, the most frequently occurring length of stress groups, words, syllables, phones), it is nearly identical in all three genres. We may therefore summarize that most frequently, prosodic phrases in Czech comprise two stress groups, three words, seven syllables, and sixteen phones. Despite these very

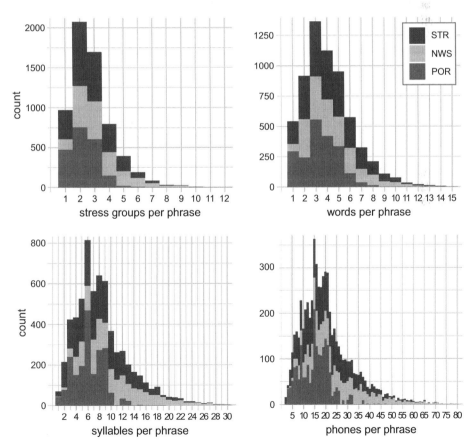

Figure 4.1: *Distribution of various phrase lengths expressed in stress groups, words, syllables, and phones in three genres (STR = storytelling, NWS = newsreading, POR = poetry reciting).*

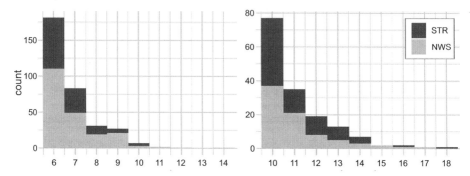

Figure 4.2: *Distribution of lengths of long phrases in two genres (STR = storytelling, NWS = newsreading) expressed in stress groups and words.*

similar modal values, it is also clear that there are differences across the three genres. Not surprisingly, long phrases are very rare in poetry reciting: the poetry dataset contains only nine phrases with six stress groups (that corresponds to less than 0.5% of the total number of prosodic phrases) and one with seven; only two phrases have more than eight words. In contrast, phrases of six or more stress groups and ten or more words are distributed relatively similarly in the STR and NWS corpora, although the longest phrases in terms of stress groups appear mostly in newsreading; these long prosodic phrases are shown in Figure 4.2 for the two genres.

Let us return to examining all three genres and their potentially significant effect on phrase length. As mentioned at the beginning of this section, we constructed generalized linear mixed-effects (GLME) models for this purpose. Several details need to be added. Since we are modelling counts (e.g., the number of stress groups per prosodic phrase), and counts tend to be not normally distributed – as is clearly visible in Figure 4.1 – we used GLMEs with Poisson regression. When phrase length is used as the dependent variable in a GLME model, with Genre defined as a fixed factor and Speaker intercept as a random factor, the effect of Genre is significant for stress groups ($\chi^2(2) = 78.04, p < 0.001$), words ($\chi^2(2) = 51.97, p < 0.001$), as well as syllables ($\chi^2(2) = 100.69, p < 0.001$); the effect plots are depicted in Figure 4.3.

First, note that the length is expressed logarithmically due to the Poisson regression modelling mentioned above; for easier interpretation, however, the absolute lengths are given at the top of the charts in grey. To examine the significance of individual comparisons, we use the confidence intervals of the emmeans, indicated by light grey bars, and especially the arrows; these are based on Tukey adjustment and serve for comparison among the emmeans confidence intervals. In other words, we can infer the significance of pairwise comparisons from the arrows. Non-overlapping arrows indicate that the given difference is statistically significant at the alpha level of 0.05: we can see this is the case in all comparisons where phrase length is expressed in (log) stress groups and syllables. However, the difference between the length of prosodic phrases in audiobooks and newsreading is not significant when expressed in words, because their confidence intervals (arrows) overlap. It is worth noting that,

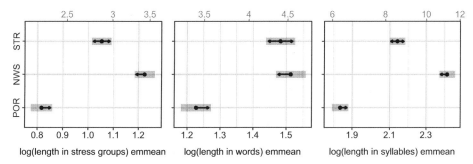

Figure 4.3: *Estimated marginal means of prosodic phrases illustrating the effect of genre (STR = storytelling, NWS = newsreading, POR = poetry reciting). Phrase length is expressed in stress groups (left), words (middle), and syllables (right), as a logarithm (absolute lengths are shown in grey at the top). Bars correspond to confidence intervals of the emmeans, and arrows serve for comparisons among them (see text).*

when expressed in words as opposed to syllables, the difference in phrase length between Czech and English also failed to reach significance (Volín, 2019; Skarnitzl & Hledíková, 2022).

It is worth returning to the longer prosodic phrases in more detail. As mentioned in section 2.3, only a major prosodic boundary including both melodic and temporal cues (i.e., BI4-type of prosodic break) is regarded in this study as ending a prosodic phrase. In other words, what has been referred to as 'a prosodic phrase' may in fact be a sequence of one or more BI3-type minor phrases, concluded by a BI4-type major prosodic break. These will henceforth be referred to as 'complex' prosodic phrases; on the other hand, phrases concluded by a major prosodic break, containing no minor phrases, will be referred to as 'unbroken' phrases. Table 4.1 shows that on average, 16% of all major prosodic phrases are complex, although the distribution is not uniform across the three genres: they are much more prevalent in newsreading (35.4%) than in storytelling (16.6%) or poetry reciting (11.1%). Newsreading thus accounts for the greatest number of complex prosodic phrases, and also for the largest number of minor breaks (with as many as four minor phrases before the last major one; see below).

Table 4.1: *Number of prosodic phrases divided according to the number of minor phrases they contain; the first line (4) refers to unbroken phrases, the remaining phrases are complex (they contain at least one BI3-type of prosodic break). STR = storytelling, NWS = newsreading, POR = poetry reciting.*

	STR	NWS	POR
4	2,112	1,329	1,808
3-4	308	376	188
3-3-4	41	78	14
3-3-3-4	2	14	0
3-3-3-3-4	0	3	0

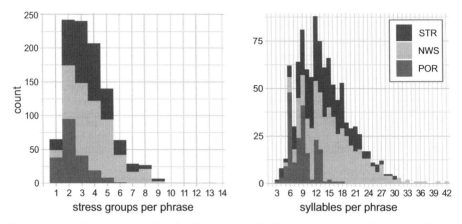

Figure 4.4: *Distribution of various lengths of complex prosodic phrases in three genres (STR = storytelling, NWS = newsreading, POR = poetry reciting) expressed in stress groups and syllables.*

It is predictable that when we survey the length of complex prosodic phrases separately, the length is considerably skewed to the right, to longer phrases, especially in STR and NWS (*cf.* Figures 4.4 and 4.1); note that the longest phrases, with very low occurrences, were not shown in Figure 4.1 because their columns would be practically invisible.

The three complex phrases which contain four minor (BI3-type) breaks are listed below. In (1), the speaker produces a list of countries, and the prosodic breaks between the constituents of the list are very weak, achieved by perceptible lengthening but no melodic changes; one could easily imagine a major (BI4) break between all of them. Examples (2) and (3) are complex sentences where the individual minor prosodic phrases are again separated using weak cues: more frequently only durational, sometimes only melodic.

(1) 'Polska | 'Maďarska | 'Estonska | 'Slovinska | a 'Kypru ‖ (speaker NF5)..., *(of) Poland | Hungary | Estonia | Slovenia | and Cyprus ‖*
(2) 'obce a 'městské 'části | 'si 'samy 'stanovují | 'kritéria 'pomocí 'kterých pak 'hodnotí | 'žadatele 'o pronájem | 'obecních 'bytů ‖ (speaker NF1)*municipalities and town districts | themselves set | criteria according to which they subsequently assess | applicants for renting | municipal flats ‖*
(3) 'si myslí | že 'do budoucna | 'by mělo 'Česko | 'o podobných 'věcech | 'vést 'debatu ‖ (speaker NF1)*(he) thinks | that in the future | Czechia should | about similar things | lead a debate ‖*

In the subsequent description, we will abandon complex prosodic phrases and only examine what we have called unbroken BI4 phrases with no minor prosodic phrase preceding them. First, we will investigate the effect of pauses on the structural properties of phrases; in other words, we are interested in finding whether phrases directly preceded and followed by another prosodic phrase (called 'internal') behave differently from those followed by a pause ('pre-pausal' phrases) and from those surrounded by pauses on both sides (called 'self-standing'). Remember that the distribution of unbroken prosodic phrases is not uniform across the three genres: as shown by the counts provided in Figure 4.5, there are fewer unbroken phrases in newsreading overall. It is obvious that newsreading stands out, with internal phrases much more prevalent than in the other two genres: our radio speakers tend to concatenate major prosodic phrases without inserting any pauses much more than STR and POR speakers. On the other hand, self-standing phrases – those surrounded by a pause on both sides – are by far the most frequent in storytelling and poetry reciting, where phrases followed by a pause (but not preceded by one) and internal phrases are represented to similar degrees.

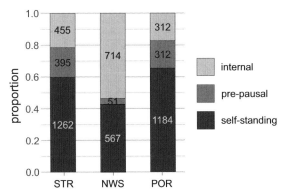

Figure 4.5: *Proportion and counts of internal, pre-pausal and self-standing major prosodic phrases in three genres (STR = storytelling, NWS = newsreading, POR = poetry reciting).*

Let us now turn to the length of prosodic phrases in the three genres depending on the presence of a pause. In this more detailed analysis, the statistical modelling becomes slightly more complicated. Poisson regression continues to be suitable for modelling phrase length in stress groups. However, since variance of the phrase length when expressed in syllables is greater than the mean value (this is called overdispersion), it is preferable to use negative binomial regression instead. Overall, GLME analysis – with the different regression methods for stress groups and syllables – reveals a significant effect of PAUSE PRESENCE on phrase length (for length in stress groups: $\chi^2(2) = 27.27$, $p < 0.001$; for length in syllables: $\chi^2(2) = 57.60$, $p < 0.001$). In addition, there is a significant interaction between PAUSE PRESENCE and GENRE (for length expressed in stress groups: $\chi^2(2) = 31.16$, $p < 0.001$; for length in syllables: $\chi^2(6) = 66.81$, $p < 0.001$). The results are displayed in the emmeans plots in Figure 4.6, for phrase length expressed in stress groups (on the left) and in syllables (on the right). Self-standing phrases are significantly longer than internal phrases in all three genres when length is expressed in stress groups: their Tukey-adjusted confidence intervals, shown as arrows, do not overlap. When expressed in syllables, this effect holds only in poetry reciting, and in newsreading as compared with the length of internal phrases. Confidence intervals for pre-pausal and internal phrases overlap in all conditions.

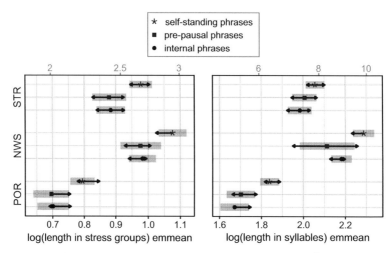

Figure 4.6: *Estimated marginal means showing the effect of the presence of pause (no pause, following pause, self-standing phrase; see text) on the length of prosodic phrases in three genres (STR = storytelling, NWS = newsreading, POR = poetry reciting) expressed in stress groups and syllables, as a logarithm (absolute lengths are shown in grey at the top). Bars correspond to confidence intervals of the emmeans, and arrows serve for comparisons among them.*

It is to be expected that the results presented above conceal a lot of individual variability. We will therefore briefly focus on the behaviour of individual speakers within the three genres. Phrase length per speaker is illustrated in Figure 4.7. It was mentioned at the beginning of this section that the typical prosodic phrase contains two stress groups. The data confirm that this applies even at the individual level, with only few exceptions. These exceptions occur mostly in newsreading (speakers NF1, NF3, NF5, NF6, NF7, and NM8) and twice in poetry reciting (speakers PF3 and PM6), and phrases of three stress groups are always more frequent in these cases. In other words, out of the 48 speakers analyzed here, only one male and five female newsreaders and one female and one male in poetry reciting produced prosodic phrases of three stress groups as most frequent. The figure also reveals that phrases with a singleton stress group are most frequent in poetry reciting, where the underlying rhythm of the poem seems to require such a solution the most. Phrases comprising a singleton stress group are rarest in newsreading.

At the other end of the scale, phrases of four or more stress groups are very rare in poetry reciting. The one phrase of six stress groups, as uttered by speaker PM1, with only 'between-word' prosodic breaks (that is, BI1-type), sounds rather like newsreading than poetry recitation:

(4) a ˈnahá ˈramena ˈz temného ˈpavučí ˈchvějivě ˈvystupují ‖ (speaker PM1) *and naked shoulders from a dark cobweb tremblingly extending* ‖

A closer examination of Figure 4.7 reveals that the division into prosodic phrases is rather uniform in poetry reciting – only speaker PF3 produced markedly fewer phrases containing one stress group and more containing three stress groups – and also in

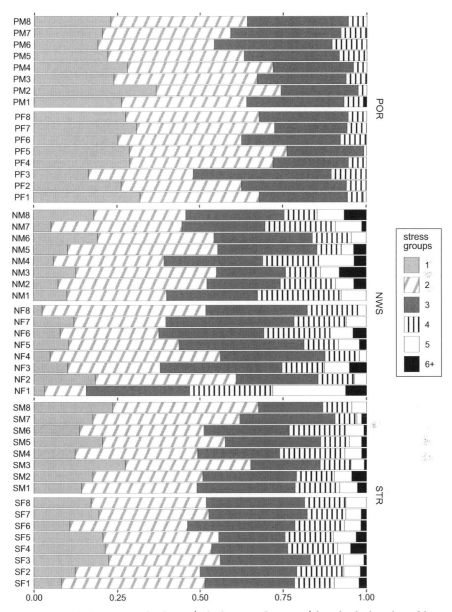

Figure 4.7: *Length of major prosodic phrases (unbroken BI4 only, see text) for individual speakers of the three genres (STR = storytelling, NWS = newsreading, POR = poetry reciting), expressed in stress groups (shortest phrases on the left, longest on the right).*

storytelling. On the other hand, there is more variability in newsreading, where two more general patterns emerge (with a prevalence of longer phrases as in speakers NF3 or NM4, and with a prevalence of shorter phrases as in speakers NF2 or NM5), and one purely individual, namely speaker NF1. In speaker NF1, prosodic phrases of one or two stress groups form a 16% minority and, conversely, phrases with five or more stress groups account for nearly 30% of all cases. An example of this speaker's phrase comprising six stress groups is provided in example (5). It is obvious that the phrase contains a lot of items of information; we assume it would be highly unlikely for such a long and information-laden stretch of speech to be realized as a single prosodic phrase by a professional newsreader.

(5) 'že je 'policisté 'použili jako 'zátaras 'v honičce 'se zločinci ‖ (speaker NF1) *that them policemen used as a barrier in a chase with criminals* ‖

This section has identified clear tendencies in the length of prosodic phrases in Czech across the three observed genres, but also relatively unsurprising between-genre differences. In Figure 4.7, we have provided a glimpse into the world of individually conditioned differences, and it is clear that such individual variation would be a worthwhile object of future research. In the following section, our description will move down a level from the prosodic phrase and analyze the length of stress groups.

4.1.2 STRESS GROUP LENGTH

The length of stress groups in the three genres is shown in Figure 4.8; length is only expressed in the number of syllables. The left part of the figure indicates that di- and trisyllabic stress groups occur most frequently in all genres and that stress groups of more than five syllables only occur in storytelling and newsreading. This is in slight contrast to previously reported results by Ondráčková (1954: 151), according to whom disyllabic stress groups were more frequent than trisyllabic ones (39% and 32%, respectively); note, however, that Ondráčková's analysis was based on prediction from a written prose text. On the other hand, Volín and Skarnitzl's (2020) analysis of six

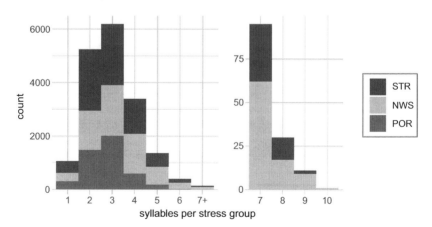

Figure 4.8: *Distribution of various stress group lengths in three genres (STR = storytelling, NWS = newsreading, POR = poetry reciting) expressed in syllables (left); length of longer stress groups in storytelling and newsreading in syllables (right).*

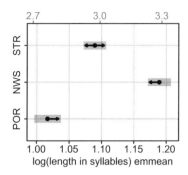

Figure 4.9: *Estimated marginal means showing the effect of genre (STR = storytelling, NWS = newsreading, POR = poetry reciting) on the length of stress groups, expressed in syllables, as a logarithm (absolute lengths are shown in grey at the top). Bars correspond to confidence intervals of the emmeans, and arrows serve for comparisons among them.*

speakers in conversational speech (who were compared with six Czech Radio newsreaders) also shows a slight prevalence of disyllabic over trisyllabic stress groups (32% vs. 26% in the spontaneous conversations). In the right part of Figure 4.8, the longer stressed groups are displayed in more detail. It is clear that newsreading features most of the longest units at the level of the stress group as well (*cf.* Figure 4.2 for the level of prosodic phrases).

When stress group length expressed in syllables is used as the dependent variable in a generalized linear mixed effects model, with Genre defined as a fixed factor and Speaker intercept as a random factor, the effect of Genre is significant ($\chi^2(2) = 72.54$, $p < 0.001$; see also Figure 4.9). The Tukey-adjusted confidence intervals, indicated by arrows in the figure, reveal that all pairwise comparisons are significant at the alpha level of 0.05, with stress groups shortest in poetry reciting and longest in newsreading.

At the phrase level, a more detailed analysis consisted in examining the effect of pause presence. At the level of the stress group, a similar 'closer' perspective can be provided by the elaborate coding of stress groups into phrase-initial, phrase-medial and phrase-final (the last featuring the nuclear melodic movement), as well as singleton-stress group phrases. The effect of genre and stress group type on the length of stress groups in our data is displayed in the emmeans plot in Figure 4.10. The figure reveals considerable between-genre differences. There is a clear interaction between Stress group type and Genre, which is confirmed as significant by a GLME analysis: $\chi^2(9) = 270.86$, $p < 0.001$. First, the tendency for stress groups to be longest in newsreading and shortest in poetry was confirmed in all positions. The situation is very similar across the three genres, with singleton and initial stress groups within each genre being longer than phrase-medial and -final stress groups.

The finding that, within each genre, phrase-initial and singleton stress groups seem to belong to the longest ones deserves further investigation. It appears that it is the initial character of the stress group that is the determining factor, which may indicate some kind of domain-initial strengthening in the temporal domain, comparable

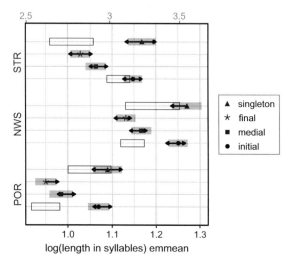

Figure 4.10: *Estimated marginal means showing the effect of stress group type and genre (STR = storytelling, NWS = newsreading, POR = poetry reciting) on the length of stress groups expressed in syllables. Bars correspond to confidence intervals of the emmeans, and arrows serve for comparisons between them. The empty rectangles show length without the contribution of anacrusis (see text).*

to articulatory strengthening of domain-initial gestures (e.g., Cho & Keating, 2009; Cho, 2016). However, stress groups classified as initial or singleton in our data may also contain unstressed syllables at the beginning, the so-called ANACRUSIS; counting such syllables as contributing to longer stress groups would not be accurate. The emmeans of length estimates without the contribution of anacrusis are also depicted in Figure 4.10, using empty rectangles alongside initial and singleton stress groups. It is obvious that initial unstressed syllables do influence the length of these stress groups considerably; without them, the effect mentioned above is essentially lost, and the initial lengthening hypothesis is thus not supported.

4.1.3 ANACRUSIS

ANACRUSIS (that is, unstressed syllables at the beginning of a prosodic phrase) has been the subject of very little empirical investigation in Czech. Traditional textbook descriptions have typically presumed that anacruses are monosyllabic (Palková, 1994: 281). In a more recent textbook, Volín and Skarnitzl (2018) explicitly allow for longer anacruses (see chapters 8 and 9 therein), but their examples were invented based on the authors' intuition, not using authentic speech.

In our dataset, phrase-initial unstressed syllables occur in all three genres and in all analyzed speakers. Figure 4.11 indicates that anacrusis is most frequent in poetry recitation, occurring in 14.3% of all stress groups, and least frequent in newsreading with 6% of stress groups featuring anacrusis; storytelling falls in between with 9.4% of stress groups beginning with anacrusis. The proportion of anacrusis is also quite stable across speakers within each genre, particularly in poetry and newsreading. While that may seem surprising in the less 'fixed' genres, it is to be expected in poetry. More specifically, iambic verses cannot be realized without anacrusis in Czech, and one of the four poems analyzed in this study is almost entirely iambic and others feature iambic elements. Some poems or their lines may allow for some variability, but other lines seem to require a particular rhythmical configuration. For example, the following line in (6) was always realized with the word *jak* (*like*) as unstressed:

(6) jak 'lovci 'rozstřílený 'dravec *like by hunters shot to pieces a bird of prey* (*like a bird of prey shot to pieces by hunters*)

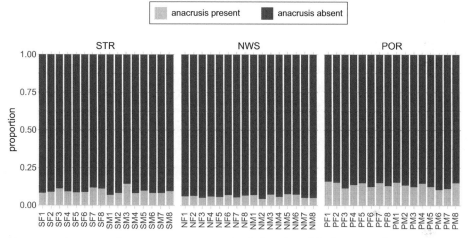

Figure 4.11: *Proportion of anacrusis occurrence in individual speakers of the three genres (STR = storytelling, NWS = newsreading, POR = poetry reciting).*

A more interesting question concerns the number of syllables in anacruses, displayed in Table 4.2 for the three genres. It is evident that a disyllabic anacrusis is not exceptional, corresponding to nearly 21% of all cases in storytelling and 29% in newsreading. At the same time, anacruses longer than one syllable are very rare in poetry recitation. We will return to the five anacruses which are made up of three syllables below.

Table 4.2: *Occurrence of mono-, di- and trisyllabic anacruses in the three genres.*

	1 syll.	2 syll.	3 syll.
STR	534	141	1
NWS	257	106	4
POR	592	21	0

It is not surprising that anacrusis most typically features grammatical words: as shown in Table 4.3, of the fifteen most frequent words, only one is lexical (*dnes*), and its relatively high frequency is given by its two occurrences in one of the poems. The conjunction *a* (*and*) is by far the most prevalent in all three genres; with 544 occurrences it accounts for nearly 33% of all instances of anacrusis. It is interesting to note that two of the fifteen most frequent anacrusis words contain two syllables: *ale* (which occurs mostly in storytelling) and *podle* (almost exclusively in newsreading). Some of the other words are also genre-specific, or more precisely specific to poetry and the four texts which were repeated by all speakers, as is clear from comparing the last three columns of the table.

Table 4.3: *The fifteen most frequent words functioning as anacrusis in total, as well as in the three genres (STR = storytelling, NWS = newsreading, POR = poetry reciting).*

Word	Total	STR	NWS	POR
a (and)	544	320	60	164
že (that)	72	31	22	19
je (is)	68	18	19	31
se (refl. pron. / with)	57	15	25	17
jak (how)	56	8	7	41
ale (but)	52	44	8	0
ten ("the" / that, masc.)	30	2	0	28
své (one's)	29	2	0	27
dnes (today)	27	0	6	21
na (on / at)	22	5	16	1
jsem (am)	19	10	0	9
ta ("the" / that, fem.)	19	3	0	16
jsou (are, 3rd ps. pl.)	18	2	2	14
ve (in)	18	0	2	16
podle (according to)	17	0	16	1

Apart from the two disyllabic anacruses listed in Table 4.3, the list would continue with various morphological variants of *který* (*which*) and with the words *jako* (*like*), *bylo* (*was, neut. sg.*) or *nebo* (*or*). Some of the disyllabic anacruses were composed of two words: e.g., *že je* (*that he/she/it is*) or *to by* (*that would*). The same applies to the trisyllabic anacruses – all five were formed by two words: *a jeho* (*and his*), *a jejich* (*and their*), *by bylo* (*would be*), and *který je* (*which / who is*) all appeared in newsreading, while *to ještě* (*that still*, in the sentence *to ještě neznamená*, *that still doesn't mean*) occurred in storytelling.

This section has demonstrated that while monosyllabic anacrusis is naturally the most frequent one, disyllabic items are by no means rare in our corpus, especially in newsreading and storytelling. Predictably, phrase-initial unstressed syllables usually correspond to grammatical words.

4.1.4 MONOSYLLABIC STRESS GROUPS

In this section, we turn to what may be seen as some sort of an opposite of anacrusis, namely to monosyllabic stress groups. We will be interested in stress groups which – at least in some cases, when they appear within a prosodic phrase and not forming a phrase on their own – defy the tendency of speakers to avoid two consecutive stressed syllables, also referred to as STRESS CLASH. The rule preventing stress clash is not particularly strict in Czech, and two consecutive stressed syllables may occur especially when they occur phrase-finally (in other words, when the two stresses occur in the last two words of a prosodic phrase) or when the semantics of the sentence seems to 'require' both words to be stressed.

Our dataset comprises 1,139 monosyllabic stress groups, with most of them occurring in storytelling (*n* = 458) and then similar number of items in newsreading (*n* = 331) and poetry (*n* = 350). One may expect most of such stress groups to be composed of lexical words. That, however, is only the case in poetry (78.6% of monosyllabic stress groups are formed by lexical words); in newsreading and storytelling the ratio is approximately 50%. A more detailed look is provided in Figure 4.12, where grammatical words are divided according to the word class in each speaker. Note that, first, the words functioning as monosyllabic adverbs in our dataset – e.g., *tak* (*so*), *tam* (*there*), *už* (*already*) – are semantically relatively empty; that is why they were not included as part of the 'lexical' group in the figure. And second, the 'word part' category was kept separately from other content words. These comprise for instance parts of names (the Burmese representative *Zo-U*, which was realized by speaker NM7 with two stresses, ['zo 'ʔu]), abbreviations (names of political parties like *ODA*, ['ʔoːdɛ: 'ʔaː]), or internet addresses (the ending .*cz* as ['t͡sɛː 'zɛt]); it is not surprising that such words occur only in newsreading.

The question of stress clash deserves investigating more thoroughly. The subsequent description will only consider storytelling and newsreading, since poetry often requires a specific prosodic rendition, and we will also disregard the word parts mentioned above. The monosyllabic stress groups may be divided into those which occur phrase-finally, as in example (7) below, and the phrase-internal ones, which are followed by another stressed syllable, with stress clash present, as in example (8). Note that the so-called RHYTHM RULE, whereby two consecutively stressed syllables in the canonical representation result in a stress shift to avoid the stress clash (Nespor & Vogel, 1986), is not applied in Czech.

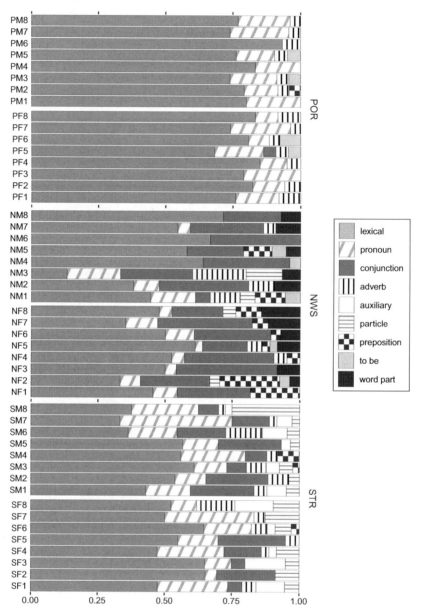

Figure 4.12: *Proportion of word types in monosyllabic stress groups produced by individual speakers of the three genres (STR = storytelling, NWS = newsreading, POR = poetry reciting).*

(7) 'ospalá | a 'chtěla 'spát ‖ (speaker SF1)*sleepy | and wanted to sleep* ‖
(8) 'jestli jsem do něj 'fakt 'zamilovaná ‖ (speaker SF4)*whether I'm with him really in love* ‖

It is also beneficial to distinguish between lexical and grammatical words in monosyllabic stress groups, because one may expect lexical words to be more prone to form

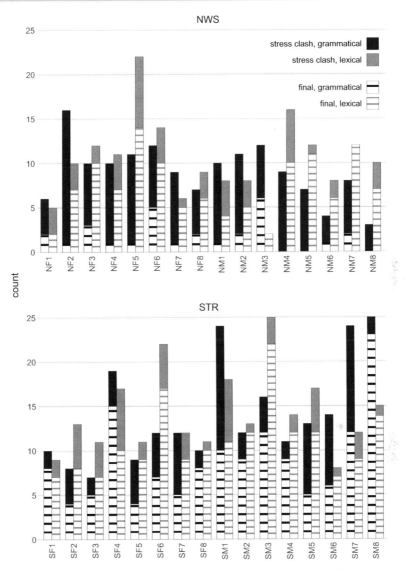

Figure 4.13: *Occurrence of monosyllabic stress groups in phrase-final positions (striped) and in stress-clash positions (solid), in lexical (grey) and grammatical (black) words; newsreading at the top, storytelling at the bottom.*

such stress groups than grammatical ones (*cf.* Palková, 1994: 282). The occurrence of all these types in newsreading and storytelling is displayed in Figure 4.13. The difference between the two genres is clear at first sight. Contrary to expectations, in newsreading stress clash occurs more frequently in grammatical words (solid black bars) than in lexical words (solid grey bars); this manifests in newsreading overall, but also in most individual speakers.

Of the 117 grammatical words in stress-clash positions, the conjunction *a* (*and*) is by far the most frequent, with 53 occurrences; *až* (*until*) and *i* (*as well as, and also*) follow with 10 and 9 occurrences, respectively. Some examples of this 'strong' conjunction *a* are provided below. In (9), there is a simple coordination which would just as likely lend itself to an unstressed realization (whether within one stress group with the previous word or as anacrusis at the beginning of the second phrase). The use of the strong form of the conjunction in example (10) – accompanied also by its long duration (over 90 ms) – seems peculiar because the two coordinated items form the title of a famous work. In fixed collocations, one would expect even a reduction of the conjunction. On the other hand, strong *a* seems more acceptable in (11) where it joins two clauses.

(9) 'ze sedumnáctého | 'a 'osumnáctého 'století: ‖ (speaker NF1) *from the 17th | and 18th century* ‖
(10) 'studie | 'násilí 'a 'metafyzika ‖ (speaker NF4) *the study | Violence and Metaphysics* ‖
(11) 'hasiči | 'likvidovali 'následky 'předchozí 'vichřice ‖ 'a 'energetici 'opravovali ... (speaker NM8) *firemen | disposed of the consequences of the previous windstorm* ‖ *and power engineers repaired ...*

In storytelling, there are 84 grammatical words in stress-clash positions, and the conjunction *a* is again most frequent, with 22 occurrences. With only one exception, the conjunction joins larger units: either two clauses, or it is located at the beginning of a sentence, as in example (12).

(12) 'za malou 'chvíli ‖ {pause} 'a 's těmito 'slovy | se 'vyřítil 'odtud ‖ (speaker SM1)... *in a little while* ‖ {pause} *and with these words, he burst out of here* ‖

Figure 4.13 also shows that the phrase-final position dominates monosyllabic stress groups in storytelling across the board (that is, in both lexical and grammatical words), while this is only the case with lexical words in newsreading. As for lexical words, there are 99 instances of stress clash in the two genres. It is numerals which seem to favour the stress clash situation, as shown in examples (13) from newsreading and (14) from storytelling; monosyllabic numerals are found in 28 of our items. Intensification is another context which favours stress clash in storytelling; this is clear from example (8) above, as well as from (15). Finally, monosyllabic first names are also likely to be realized as stressed, despite stress clash, as shown in (16).

(13) 'prověřují 'kriminalisté 'dva 'muže ‖ (speaker NF5) *are checking investigators two men* ‖
(14) 'a měl 'dvě 'děti ‖ (speaker SF2) *and (he) had two children* ‖
(15) 'bylo to 'dost 'mrzuté ‖ (speaker SM6) *it was quite annoying* ‖
(16) 'George 'Bush | a 'John 'Kerry ‖ (speaker NM4) *George Bush | and John Kerry* ‖

4.1.5 DISCUSSION

The aim of this section was to examine the internal structure of prosodic phrases. As summarized in Table 4.4, Czech prosodic phrases most frequently (that is, as the modal value) contain two stress groups, three words, and seven syllables. Since the length values are skewed to the right (see the histograms in Figures 4.1 and 4.2), the mean values are slightly higher. Our data show that phrases extending ten stress groups, fifteen words, and thirty syllables are highly exceptional.

Table 4.4: *Summary of modal and mean length of prosodic phrases in the three genres (STR = storytelling, NWS = newsreading, POR = poetry reciting), expressed in stress groups, words, and syllables.*

	Stress groups		Words		Syllables	
	Mode	Mean	Mode	Mean	Mode	Mean
STR	2	2.56	3	3.96	7	7.64
NWS	2	2.78	3	3.72	7	9.25
POR	2	2.14	3	3.25	6	5.98

The results of the analyses point to various factors which affect phrase length. First of all, it is naturally the genre, with phrases being shortest in poetry recitation and longest in newsreading; this relationship is also supported at the level of stress groups. Second, the prosodic complexity of the phrases also plays a significant role, with the longest phrases belonging to what we refer to as complex phrases (see Figure 4.4), in contrast to unbroken phrases. Furthermore, Figure 4.7 hinted at individual differences in phrase length within each genre; to this we might add that professionalism also seems to play a role. Volín (2019) reported that professional newsreaders' prosodic phrases were 10.8 syllables long on average (i.e., slightly more than in our, larger dataset), while nonprofessional speakers' newsreading yielded phrases of 12.9 syllables on average. The presence of pause also influences phrase length, with self-standing phrases (i.e., those surrounded by a pause on both sides) being the longest.

The more detailed analyses presented in Sections 4.1.3 and 4.1.4 revealed an interesting fact about the conjunction *a* (*and*). This word turned out to be by far the most frequent one functioning as anacrusis (i.e., unstressed syllable at the beginning of a prosodic phrase). Specifically, *a* accounts for nearly 33% of all instances of anacrusis. Of course, this is hardly surprising; however, it is remarkable that the conjunction *a* also constituted the most frequent monosyllabic stress group (8.4%). In addition, when we narrow monosyllabic stress groups down to those with stress clash (i.e., featuring two consecutive stressed syllables), *a* accounts for over 37% of all stress clash instances in grammatical words; note that this value differs from that given in the previous section because POR items were not included there. A detailed acoustic analysis would be necessary to identify factors which contribute to the conjunction *a* being produced as anacrusis (that is, unstressed) or a monosyllabic stress group. However, our repeated listening – which was required to make the perceptually based decisions for the purpose of this study – has rather shown that no clearcut acoustic boundaries can be stipulated. Whether or not a word is heard as prominent always depends on the broader phonetic context of the given prosodic phrase and on the interplay of all prosodic parameters simultaneously. Put differently, the same acoustic qualities of (not only) the conjunction *a* may result in the perception of anacrusis in one phrase and of a stressed syllable in another.

4.2 PROSODIC PHRASE ACOUSTICALLY

This section will present acoustic analyses which pertain to the level of the prosodic phrase. We will be interested in the change of various acoustic (or more precisely, prosodic) parameters throughout phrases. The change will be expressed as a slope of the acoustic values. This may be easiest to exemplify on intonation downtrends, which were mentioned in Section 1.3: fundamental frequency will fluctuate within the phrase depending on, among others, its prosodic structure and semantic content but, overall, it is likely to demonstrate a global downward trend, a gradual decrease in the height of comparable melodic events. Such a trend will be measured for all the acoustic parameters analyzed in this study; naturally, the trend may be decreasing as in the case of fundamental frequency, but also increasing; for example, a parameter which reflects the degree of breathiness of vowels would be likely to grow toward the end of many prosodic phrases. In the subsequent sections, we will focus on the three primary prosodic features – fundamental frequency (4.2.1), intensity (4.2.2), and duration (4.2.3) – and also on voice quality (4.2.4).

The slope of acoustic values is calculated as the least-square linear fit of the extracted acoustic values; all computations were implemented using R. In prosodic analysis, there is always the question of which measurement points should be used. The choice of measurement points must of course be consistent throughout the analyzed material and should ideally be linguistically sensible. To meet the latter requirement, we applied four approaches that differ in which data points from the entire contour were used for fitting the linear slope. These four approaches are exemplified on a fundamental frequency (f_0) contour in Figure 4.14 and defined as follows:

all-point – all points of a contour serve as input into the regression analysis,
syllable nuclei – only points located in syllable nuclei (vowels or syllabic consonants) are used, represented by the values of three neighbouring points in the midpoint of the segment,
stressed nuclei – only points in stressed syllable nuclei are used, represented in the same way as in the previous approach,
nuclear syllable nuclei – we also examined the slope in the nuclear portion of the phrase only, based on the syllable nuclei approach.

To be able to measure the slope of acoustic parameters reliably, we only considered prosodic phrases of at least two stress groups. All boxplot figures are created using the *ggplot2* package in R and show a 98%-quantile range of values of the given acoustic parameter; in other words, 2% of the most extreme outlier values are not visualized.

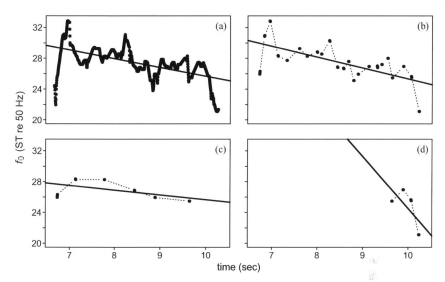

Figure 4.14: *Illustration of the four approaches to the quantification of slope: all-point (a), syllable nuclei (b), stressed nuclei (c), and nuclear syllable nuclei (d).*

For statistical analyses, we constructed linear mixed-effects (LME) models using R and the *lme4* package. The given acoustic parameter served as the dependent variable. There were three fixed effects – GENRE (STR, NWS and POR), PAUSE PRESENCE (internal, pre-pausal and self-standing), and EXTRACTION METHOD (all-point, syllable nuclei, stressed nuclei, nuclear syllable nuclei) – and SPEAKER as random intercept.

Residual plots were visually inspected for deviations from normality and homoscedasticity. The significance of individual fixed effects was tested by comparing the full model to a reduced model with the given factor excluded using likelihood ratio tests. Plots showing mean values of the measured variables and their confidence intervals were created using the *emmeans* package and visualized with *ggplot2*. For every combination of acoustic parameter and extraction method, we removed 2% of the most extreme outlier values for a more transparent visualization; note that this is a slightly different procedure than for the boxplots mentioned above, where 98% of all data (that is, of all the slopes shown in one plot) were depicted.

4.2.1 FUNDAMENTAL FREQUENCY

For the extraction of fundamental frequency (f_0) contours, we used YAAPT (Zahorian & Hu, 2008) with f_0 detection in the 60–600 Hz range, using both temporal and spectral domain processing for highest accuracy, and keeping the voiced/unvoiced decision on. Based on subsequent visual inspection of the extracted values in a histogram, a new f_0 minimum and maximum was determined for each speaker and the f_0 extraction process was run again, with the aim to eliminate octave jumps or erroneously detected values (for instance in noise segments). Since YAAPT runs in the Matlab environment, the mPraat toolbox (Bořil & Skarnitzl, 2016) was used to save PitchTiers, objects which are interpretable in the Praat programme (Boersma & Weenink, 2023). The f_0 contours were then converted to the perceptually interpretable semitone (ST) scale and related to 50 Hz, and finally interpolated by a 3-ms step using the rPraat package (Bořil & Skarnitzl, 2016).

We will first examine overall slopes of f_0 using boxplots. In Figure 4.15 (as well as in subsequent boxplots illustrating the slope of acoustic parameters), if f_0 were not to differ between beginnings and ends of prosodic phrases (that is, if no downward or upward slope were to be observed), the boxplots would be centred around the slope value of 0 ST/second with a very narrow range. That is clearly not the case in our data. Since the boxes encompass 50% of the data (between the first and third quartile, Q1 and Q3), the figure indicates that f_0 slopes are in most cases negative, meaning f_0 decreases throughout the phrase – that is of course not a surprising finding. However, there are also prosodic phrases with positive slopes, as shown by the whiskers (extending from the boxes) and outliers (symbolized by individual dots); note again that the most extreme outlier values are not visualized, as mentioned above.

Let us examine all the relationships shown in the boxplot, first of all the role of genre. We can see that the most steeply falling f_0 slopes can be observed in poetry reciting: all Q3–Q1 boxes are located in the negative values; note also the conspicuous absence of outliers in POR above 7 ST/s in the first two extraction methods. In storytelling and newsreading, the slopes of f_0 are slightly less negative. It is especially in these two genres that the effect of pause presence is visible: while the slope of internal prosodic phrases (those flanked by speech activity on both sides) is more or less centred around zero, phrases in the pre-pausal position and in particular self-standing phrases (flanked by pauses on both sides) manifest a higher number of falling f_0 slopes. In other words, the more a prosodic phrase is surrounded by pauses, the steeper the melodic slope tends to be observed.

The proportion of negative f_0 slopes in the individual conditions is summarized in Table 4.5. The prevalence of declining gradients is obvious in all conditions and occurs mostly in self-standing phrases and in poetry reciting. Finally, as for the effect of extraction methods, the results shown in Figure 4.15 point to no systematic difference between extracting f_0 values in all nuclei, stressed nuclei only, or the computationally easiest all-point method. (Note that Table 4.5 and the other summarizing tables in this section will show data for only one of the extraction methods – typically from all syllable nuclei – for easier orientation.)

Figure 4.15 displayed the first three extraction methods mentioned above. We now turn to the fourth one, where f_0 slope is examined in the nuclear portion of each prosodic phrase; it would not be surprising to find steeper melodic slopes here, since this is where the nuclear pitch movement is realized. That is exactly what we can see in Figure 4.16; notice that the range of the vertical axis is much larger than in the previous figure. Storytelling manifests the steepest negative slopes, particularly in self-standing phrases. It

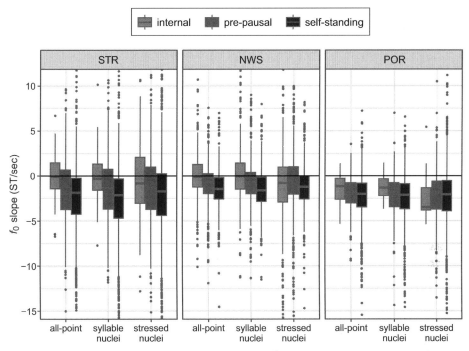

Figure 4.15: *Fundamental frequency slopes in the three genres (STR = storytelling, NWS = newsreading, POR = poetry reciting), depending on the presence of pauses, extracted in all points, in all syllable nuclei, and in stressed nuclei only.*

Table 4.5. *Percentage of negative f_0 gradients extracted in syllable nuclei in the three genres (STR = storytelling, NWS = newsreading, POR = poetry reciting), depending on the presence of pauses.*

	Internal	Pre-pausal	Self-standing
STR	54.2	66.8	79.1
NWS	51.5	67.3	78.4
POR	77.8	86.8	87.6

should be pointed out that an f_0 drop of 10 or more semitones is unlikely to happen: slope values are related to time (one second), and the nuclear portions of phrases will usually be shorter. Moreover, the figure shows, across the three genres, a greater proportion of positive slopes in the nuclear part of internal phrases; this is probably related to the fact that internal phrases are most likely to contain continuation rises.

Let us now apply the statistical procedures mentioned above and observe the effects from the viewpoint of statistical significance. The results are shown in Figure 4.17. The effect of all the three fixed factors is statistically significant (for GENRE, $\chi^2(2) = 12.57$,

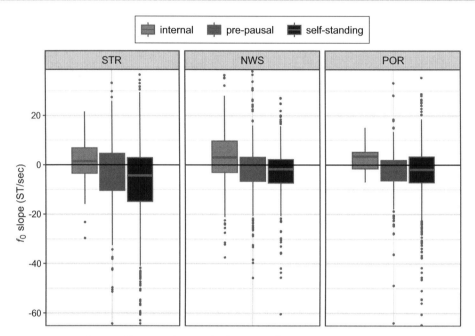

Figure 4.16: *Fundamental frequency slopes in the three genres (STR = storytelling, NWS = newsreading, POR = poetry reciting), depending on the presence of pauses, extracted in the syllable nuclei of the nuclear portion of each prosodic phrase.*

$p = 0.002$; for extraction method, $\chi^2(3) = 136.58$, $p < 0.001$; for pause presence, $\chi^2(2) = 143.65$, $p < 0.001$). The arrows in each plot inform about the significance of individual pairwise comparisons, capturing the confidence intervals of the respective emmean. Specifically, when the two arrows overlap, the difference in f_0 slopes does not reach statistical significance at the alpha level of 0.05. Conversely, when the arrows do not overlap, the difference between the two conditions is regarded as statistically significant. The light grey rectangles correspond to the second kind of confidence intervals which inform us about the significance with respect to a specific value (0 ST/sec in this case) rather than about the significance of individual pairwise comparisons.

The plot confirms that the steepest melodic downtrends are in storytelling and the shallowest in newsreading, with the difference between the two being statistically significant. However, poetry reciting did not differ significantly from either of the other genres. On the whole, however, we can reject the null hypothesis that no slope occurs in our speakers, because the light grey rectangles are all located below zero. Regarding the extraction methods, we can see that only the nuclear method differs significantly from the others. Overall, all methods yield significantly negative slopes, as indicated by the rectangle confidence intervals. Finally, for PAUSE PRESENCE, the non-overlapping arrows show that all pairwise comparisons reach significance. As mentioned above, internal prosodic phrases manifest the largest proportion of positive f_0 slopes, which is reflected in Figure 4.17 by the rectangle confidence interval including the zero value.

4. PROSODIC PHRASE IN CONTEMPORARY CZECH

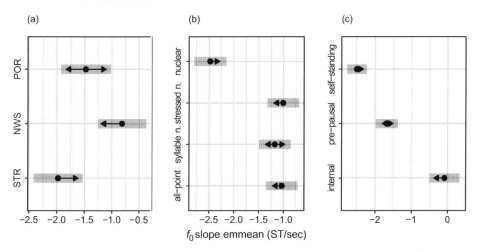

Figure 4.17: *Estimated marginal means of fundamental frequency slopes illustrating the effect of (a) the three genres (STR = storytelling, NWS = newsreading, POR = poetry reciting), (b) extraction method, and (c) pause presence.*

Let us turn to some individual phrases. We will first illustrate typical behaviour of f_0 slope and then examine some of the more peripheral values, always trying to provide some interesting information concerning the linguistic makeup of the phase, some contextual factors or information related to the extraction method that was used. Figure 4.18 shows an example of a typical melodic slope, taken from storytelling (speaker SF3): f_0 was extracted from all syllable nuclei, and the regression line (the thicker line) drops by −1.68 semitones per second (the scale of the right vertical axis is kept constant in all these figures for easier comparison). The transcription indicates that this is an example of a complex phrase (see Section 4.1), made up of a minor phrase (*poprvé*) and then a major one. It is interesting to note that the linear approximation is a surprisingly good fit for the interpolated contour: the speaker really fell more or

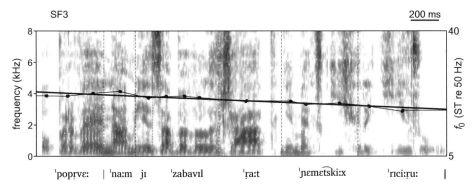

Figure 4.18: *A typical f_0 slope, based on extraction from syllable nuclei (black dots), shown as the thick regression line (see text concerning the missing value in the last word).*

less continuously throughout the complex phrase with her voice, and the entire drop amounted to nearly 5 ST over the 3-second phrase. However, notice that no f_0 value was provided by the extractor in the last syllable; if it had been extracted correctly, it is conceivable that it would lie well below the regression line.

The following example in Figure 4.19 illustrates how large the effect of extraction method may be. In this short phrase of two stress groups taken from poetry reciting, the speaker produces the first syllable [po] with a remarkably high melodic accent at about 320 Hz, while all the remaining syllables (the first in anacrusis, as well as the remaining syllables) oscillate between 200 and 220 Hz. This is a jump of over 6 ST, more than half an octave. This can be captured in different ways. When only stressed syllable nuclei (that is, [po] and [gro]) are used to express the slope of fundamental frequency, it amounts to −16.28 ST/sec (black solid line). However, if we were to extract the slope based on all syllable nuclei – that is, crucially, including the 218 Hz (25.5 ST re 50 Hz) value in the nucleus of the unstressed word *ten* – the slope would be much more moderate, though still steeper than average, with −3.81 ST/sec.

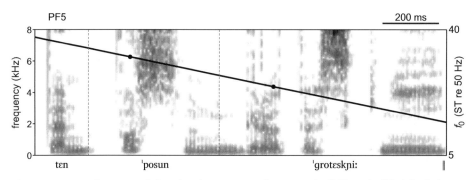

Figure 4.19: *A steeply negative f_0 slope, based on extraction from stressed syllable nuclei (black dots), shown as the thick regression line.*

Finally, let us examine in more detail one of the positive f_0 slopes. It will not be surprising that such slopes occur mostly in sentence-internal clauses or, more rarely, in questions (especially in storytelling or poetry reciting). Figure 4.20 presents an example of the former, taken from newsreading, where the speaker begins his broadcast by saying *Je středa* (*It's Wednesday*) and continues with the specific date (*October 13* in that specific broadcast). The positive slope of 15.81 ST/sec is achieved mostly by the upward melodic step between the copular verb *je* (90 Hz) and the following stressed syllable (132 Hz), creating a difference of over 6.5 ST. Note that this short phrase exemplifies stress clash discussed in Section 4.1.4; the verb *je* could easily have been pronounced unstressed, as anacrusis.

The last perspective that we will provide is that of the individual speakers. Individual behaviour in speech sciences is always interesting: it helps us understand how speakers realize their goals in communication. Analyses of individual speakers will

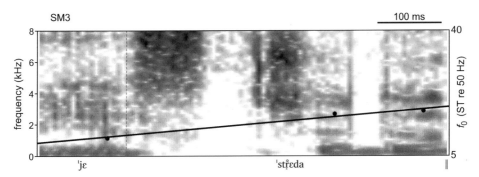

Figure 4.20: *A positive f_0 slope, based on extraction from syllable nuclei (black dots), shown as the thick regression line.*

be based on self-standing phrases only, due to the lower occurrence of internal and pre-pausal phrases at least in some of the genres (see Figure 4.5 in Section 4.1). The boxplots in Figure 4.21 depict f_0 slopes of individual speakers, ordered from highest to lowest within each genre. With the exception of speaker SM8 in storytelling and speakers NM5 and NF4 in newsreading, there is a clear prevalence of negative gradients, corresponding to falling intonation within prosodic phrases. No clear picture emerges when we want to analyze the effect of speaker sex. However, female and male speakers do seem to behave somewhat differently within the three genres: shallower f_0 gradients can be observed in four of the eight female newsreaders, and six males manifested the steepest slopes in poetry reciting.

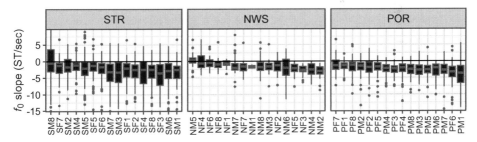

Figure 4.21: *Fundamental frequency slopes in individual speakers of the three genres (STR = storytelling, NWS = newsreading, POR = poetry reciting), extracted in syllable nuclei.*

4.2.2 INTENSITY

The intensity contour of each prosodic phrase was extracted in Praat, using the default parameters except for minimum f_0 which was set to 70 Hz; this resulted in an analysis window of 14 ms. Praat's Intensity object was then converted into an IntensityTier, whose contour was subsequently interpolated by a 3-ms step using the rPraat package.

Boxplots corresponding to intensity slopes in the three genres, extracted using the three approaches listed above, are shown in Figure 4.22. There are several points worth mentioning. First, a clear downward tendency appears within each triplet which reflects the presence of pauses: intensity slopes tend to be more negative in self-standing prosodic phrases (those surrounded by pauses) and most shallow or even slightly positive in internal phrases (which are surrounded on both sides by speech, by neighbouring prosodic phrases). In other words, intensity drops more between the beginning and end of self-standing phrases and remains similar within longer speaking turns; a similar tendency regarding fundamental frequency was observed in the previous section. Second, if we compare the three extraction methods, the sharpest negative downtrend may be observed when intensity is extracted from the syllable nuclei. Finally, as for the effect of genre, the steepest intensity slopes are visible in poetry reciting, and slightly shallower slopes can be seen in storytelling. Interestingly, practically no negative slopes are observed in newsreading; this may be due to dynamic compression in radio broadcasting, but we have no knowledge of whether and to what extent dynamic compression was applied. In fact, it is conceivable that dynamic compression may have been applied even in storytelling. We will return to the issue of dynamic compression toward the end of this section.

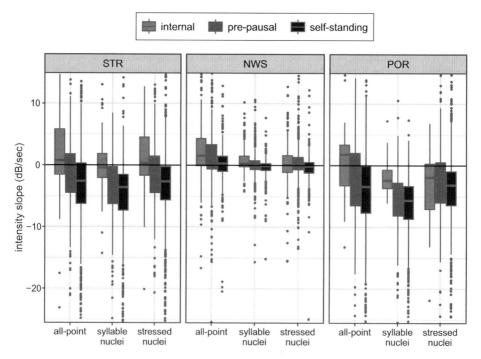

Figure 4.22: *Intensity slopes in the three genres (STR = storytelling, NWS = newsreading, POR = poetry reciting), depending on the presence of pauses, extracted in all points, in all syllable nuclei, and in stressed nuclei only.*

The most important tendencies are summarized in Table 4.6, which shows the percentage of declining intensity gradients in the individual conditions. The table confirms that it is only in self-standing prosodic phrases that falling intensity slopes are visible in all genres, and most of them occur in poetry reciting. On the other hand, most internal phrases in newsreading demonstrate a growing intensity slope, as discussed above.

Table 4.6: *Percentage of negative intensity gradients extracted in syllable nuclei in the three genres (STR = storytelling, NWS = newsreading, POR = poetry reciting), depending on the presence of pauses.*

	Internal	Pre-pausal	Self-standing
STR	58.3	78.0	89.9
NWS	34.8	47.6	59.4
POR	81.5	93.0	95.7

Next, we focus specifically on the nuclear portion of prosodic phrases, using the approach dubbed 'nuclear syllable nuclei' above. Specifically, we are interested in finding out whether the tendencies visible in Figure 4.22 become more pronounced when we consider only the nuclear portion of prosodic phrases (that is, in our material, the part from the last stressed syllable of the phrase until its end). In Figure 4.23, note that the scale of the intensity slope axis is much larger than in the previous figure. It is clear that, while intensity gradients still oscillate around the zero value in newsreading, they are considerably more negative in storytelling and poetry reciting, and that there is much more variability in the data. Remember, however, that the negative values do not mean that an actual drop in intensity of 50 or 70 dB is ever achieved: the slopes are expressed in decibels per second, and the nuclear portions of prosodic phrases are typically much shorter than one second.

Linear mixed effects modelling shows that the effect of all three fixed factors is statistically significant (see Figure 4.24). For GENRE, $\chi^2(2) = 71.00$, $p < 0.001$, and all pairwise comparisons are significant. In other words, intensity slope is significantly steeper in poetry reciting than in storytelling, where it is in turn significantly steeper than in newsreading. In addition, since the newsreading light grey rectangle confidence interval overlaps with the zero value, we cannot reject the hypothesis that intensity significantly declines in newsreading, confirming the tendencies observed in the boxplots above. For EXTRACTION METHOD, $\chi^2(3) = 3128.46$, $p < 0.001$; only the difference between the all-point and stressed nuclei method failed to reach significance. The effect of PAUSE PRESENCE is also significant ($\chi^2(2) = 139.04$, $p < 0.001$), with all pairwise comparisons yielding significant differences.

As in the previous section, we will now examine several individual cases. As mentioned above, our newsreaders manifested different intensity trends than the professional actors in storytelling or students in poetry reciting. Typical intensity slopes

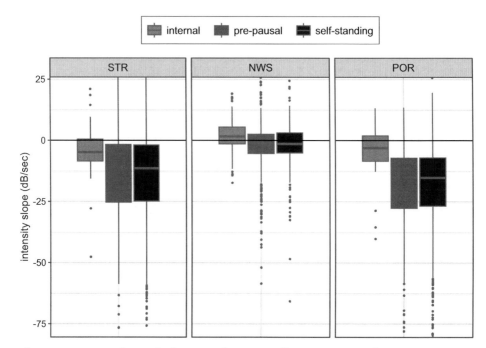

Figure 4.23: *Intensity slopes in the three genres (STR = storytelling, NWS = newsreading, POR = poetry reciting), depending on the presence of pauses, extracted in the syllable nuclei of the nuclear portion of each prosodic phrase.*

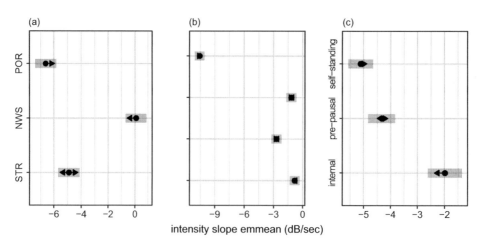

Figure 4.24: *Estimated marginal means of intensity slopes illustrating the effect of (a) the three genres (STR = storytelling, NWS = newsreading, POR = poetry reciting), (b) extraction method, and (c) pause presence.*

are compared in Figure 4.25 for newsreading (in the top panel) and for the other two genres (in the bottom panel). The slightly rising intensity in newsreading is nicely captured by the regression line, which manifests a gradient of 2.44 dB/sec. In the bottom panel, the linear fit to the intensity curve, with its negative slope of −3.52 dB/sec, may be regarded as less straightforward but still not difficult to observe. The intensity drop in the last word, přeci, is particularly well visible in the spectrogram.

An unusually steep negative gradient of intensity is illustrated on a prosodic phrase from storytelling in Figure 4.26. It consists of two stress groups (notice the three monosyllabic words functioning as enclitics). The regression line shows that the negative slope of −25.82 dB/sec is largely determined by the extreme values of the intensity curve. The maximum happens to be located near the beginning of the prosodic phrase: the stressed syllable [nɛ] is pronounced very strongly, which can be ascertained from the very prominent F2 and F3 of the vowel. The minimum is located at the end of the phrase, in the closure of the voiceless plosive [t]; the release of the [t] is very weak and does not change the slope of the regression line too much.

An opposite direction of the intensity gradient is clear in another phrase from storytelling, shown in Figure 4.27. To a certain extent, the strongly rising trend of 25.58 dB/sec is present due to the phrase-initial [t], but intensity would grow consid-

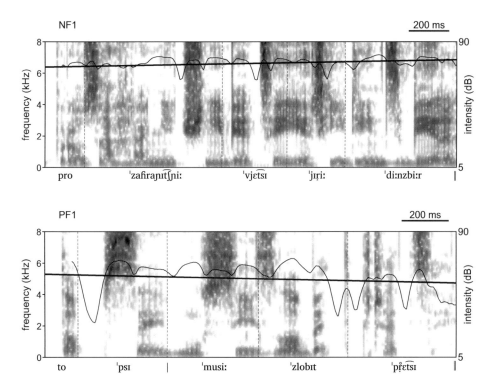

Figure 4.25: *A typical intensity slope for newsreading (top) and for poetry reciting and storytelling (bottom), based on extraction from all points (the thin curve), shown as the thick regression line.*

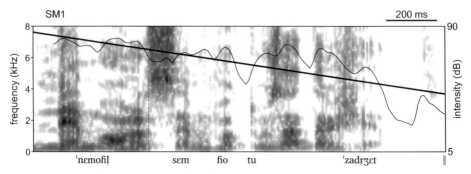

Figure 4.26: *A steeply negative intensity slope, based on extraction from all points of the intensity contour (thin curve), shown as the thick regression line.*

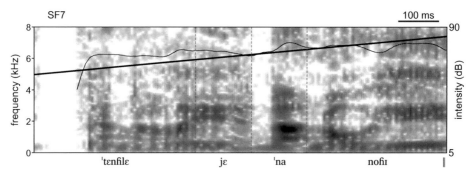

Figure 4.27: *A steeply positive intensity slope, based on extraction from all points of the intensity contour (thin curve), shown as the thick regression line.*

erably even without it, and the loudness increase is clearly perceptible in this phrase – and again reflected in the strong formants of the final stress group's vowels.

Finally, we will present one of the extreme examples in the nuclear portion of a prosodic phrase – so extreme, in fact, that it does not appear in Figure 4.23 at all (as mentioned at the beginning of Section 4.2, the most extreme outlier values are not visualized in the boxplots). The intensity gradient of 70.02 dB/sec in Figure 4.28 looks staggering, but one must understand that this increase is realized on the two last syllables of the phrase, on the word *čekal*. Given the distance between the syllable nuclei of slightly less than 200 milliseconds, the actual intensity difference between the two vowels is about 13 dB. That is still a lot, and it is worth commenting on the reason. The phrase corresponds to a question (the meaning is *How long did he wait here?*), so high intensity at its end is not surprising. What is surprising is the low intensity of the stressed syllable. The resolution of this 'conundrum' is provided by the spectrogram: we can see that the 'stressed' /ɛ/ is in fact very weak, with three low-amplitude glottal pulses and a vowel quality approaching the mid central [ə]; for easier comparison, see the spectrogram as well as the waveform of this word in Figure 4.29. Centralization – and overall reduced realization – of a stressed vowel may sound like an oxymoron

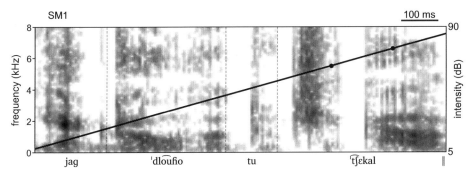

Figure 4.28: *A steeply positive intensity slope, based on extraction in the syllable nuclei of the nuclear portion (black dots), shown as the thick regression line.*

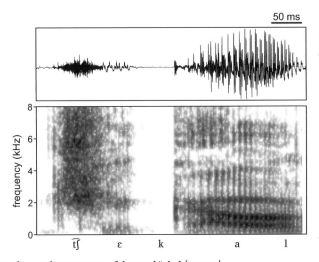

Figure 4.29: *Waveform and spectrogram of the word čekal (see text).*

to many readers, but although vowel quality does not systematically differ between stressed and unstressed syllables (in either direction; see Skarnitzl, 2018), this is not unheard of in Czech; empirical evidence as to how frequent this phenomenon is in ordinary speech, however, is lacking.

Let us again examine the behaviour of the individual speakers. Intensity slopes of all speakers in self-standing phrases, ordered from the shallowest to the steepest, are shown in Figure 4.30. At the beginning of this section, we discussed the possibility of dynamic compression being applied on radio broadcasting and possibly also when recording audio books in professional studios. If we were to draw a conclusion based on the data in this plot, we would suggest that such compression indeed was applied in newsreading: we can see that the variability of intensity slopes is markedly lower in newsreading and centred around zero. There are a few speakers whose intensity slopes are overall negative, but still to a very low extent. It seems logical that radio broadcast-

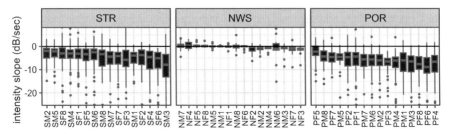

Figure 4.30: *Intensity slopes in individual speakers of the three genres (STR = storytelling, NWS = newsreading, POR = poetry reciting), extracted in syllable nuclei.*

ers' loudness should not oscillate too much, as this may lower their intelligibility. On the other hand, intensity gradients in storytelling by professional actors and in poetry reciting by students are quite comparable, the outlying values reaching well below −10 dB/sec. Dynamic compression is therefore unlikely to have been applied on the actors' speech.

4.2.3 DURATION

Expressing slopes in the temporal domain may seem somewhat less straightforward and intuitive. Measuring the duration of individual speech segments and reporting absolute values would not be very helpful. To make values of absolute duration more interpretable, some kind of normalization would be necessary which would account for inherent durations of various sounds, the prosodic context, and other factors (see Volín & Skarnitzl, 2007). However, applying such an approach in this study is impossible given the size of our speech corpora. Here, it seemed preferable to move from the level of segments to the level of syllables. Specifically, we measured temporal distances of midpoints between syllable nuclei, as defined in the following formulas:

$$t = \left[t_{nucleus}(1), \frac{t_{nucleus}(1) + t_{nucleus}(2)}{2}, \ldots, \frac{t_{nucleus}(n-1) + t_{nucleus}(n)}{2}, t_{nucleus}(n) \right]$$

where $t_{(1\ldots n)}$ corresponds to the times of individual syllabic nuclei. These temporal distances are then used to calculate syllable durations:

$$dur_{syll} = [t_2 - t_1, \ldots, t_n - t_{n-1}]$$

Given our purpose – to express the duration trend using a regression line – this is a reasonable and computationally efficient approximation of syllable duration. Due to this calculation, Figure 4.31 only displays the corresponding two extraction methods – syllable nuclei and stressed nuclei. As was the case in the previous analyses, the resulting temporal contour was then interpolated by a 3-ms step using rPraat.

In the boxplots shown in Figure 4.31, the duration slope value of 0 would mean that, overall, speakers were not slowing down or speeding up over the course of a prosodic phrase. Negative values of duration slope refer to faster speech rate within a phrase (i.e., decreasing duration), while positive values correspond to slower rate (growing duration). The results illustrated in the boxplots are quite interesting when it comes to the three genres. We can see that most of the datapoints in newsreading are below 0, indicating a gradual speeding up of the newsreaders in our dataset. That may seem counterintuitive: one may expect increasing duration (which would reflect final deceleration), just as previous sections have documented a declining trend of fundamental frequency and intensity. However, within the three genres examined here, it is exactly radio newsreading – with its inherent pressure to communicate a large amount of information in a short span of time – where gradual speeding up throughout prosodic phrases seems sensible. In contrast, duration slopes in poetry reciting are located around the zero value. In other words, speech rate seems to remain relatively constant throughout prosodic phrases in the analyzed poems, which is something that the rhythm of reciting poems may 'enforce'. Finally, storytelling manifests the greatest proportion of positive slope values, that is the greatest proportion of slowing down between the beginning and end of prosodic phrases. Figure 4.31 also shows a weak effect

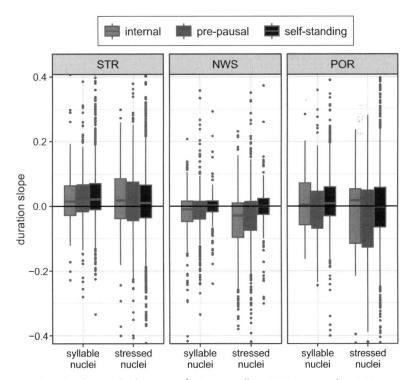

Figure 4.31: *Duration slopes in the three genres (STR = storytelling, NWS = newsreading, POR = poetry reciting), depending on the presence of pauses, extracted in all syllable nuclei and in stressed nuclei only.*

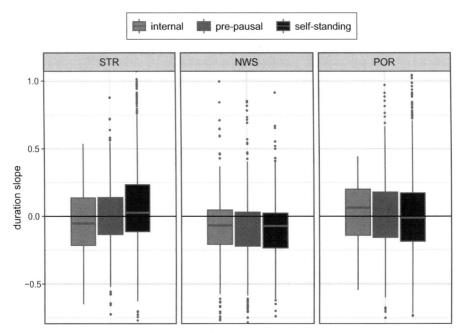

Figure 4.32: *Duration slopes in the three genres (STR = storytelling, NWS = newsreading, POR = poetry reciting), depending on the presence of pauses, extracted in the syllable nuclei of the nuclear portion of each prosodic phrase.*

of pause presence: in most of the conditions, duration slope seems to be slightly less variable in self-standing phrases. The two extraction methods differ little, with duration slopes based on stressed syllables showing, not surprisingly, greater variability compared to slopes computed from all syllables.

It is worth examining the nuclear portions of prosodic phrases separately. As can be seen in Figure 4.32, the acceleration for newsreading mentioned above seems even greater when considered from the last stressed syllable until the end of the phrase, with the Q3–Q1 boxes located almost entirely in negative values.

Table 4.7 presents a concise summary confirming the relationships both for the entire phrases (on the left in each cell) and for their nuclear portions (on the right); note that the table shows the proportion of positive duration gradients (i.e., increasing duration, deceleration). With the exception of poetry reciting, the table indicates that deceleration is manifested to a larger extent in the more 'global' perspective of a prosodic phrase than in the 'local' view of its nuclear portion, which seems counterintuitive: one would expect precisely the last stress group to be the most important domain of deceleration.

Let us examine the statistical significance of the observed differences using LME. As with the previous two parameters, the effect of all three fixed factors on duration slopes is significant (for GENRE, $\chi^2(2) = 34.37$, $p < 0.001$; for EXTRACTION METHOD, $\chi^2(3) = 55.69$, $p < 0.001$; for PAUSE PRESENCE, $\chi^2(2) = 25.90$, $p < 0.001$). The results are

Table 4.7: *Percentage of positive duration gradients extracted in syllable nuclei in the three genres (STR = storytelling, NWS = newsreading, POR = poetry reciting), depending on the presence of pauses. Within each cell, values for the entire phrase / values in the nuclear portion.*

	Internal	Pre-pausal	Self-standing
STR	62.5 / 40.3	62.8 / 50.6	67.2 / 55.6
NWS	39.8 / 36.9	41.0 / 32.4	52.7 / 31.1
POR	51.9 / 51.9	47.4 / 51.8	56.5 / 48.7

shown in Figure 4.33. All pairwise comparisons between genres are significant at the alpha level of 0.05 and, crucially, we can see that the rectangle confidence interval is below 0 in newsreading (indicating significant acceleration), includes 0 in poetry reciting, and lies above 0 in storytelling (indicating significant deceleration). Regarding the extraction method, it is visible that the difference between the all-point and syllable nuclei method is not significant, whereas all other pairwise comparisons are. Finally, the duration slope in self-standing phrases is significantly different from that in internal or pre-pausal phrases.

We will now examine several individual cases. In the description above, we mentioned final deceleration (often referred to in literature as final lengthening). This is manifested in positive duration gradients, and two examples from the same speaker, a professional actor, are shown in Figure 4.34. Duration values were extracted only from the nuclei of stressed syllables, but the slope would differ relatively little if all syllables were considered. It is especially in the second example, with its slope of 0.51, where the last stressed syllable plays an enormous role; it contains a phonologically

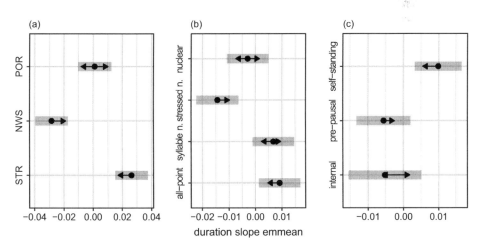

Figure 4.33: *Estimated marginal means of duration slopes illustrating the effect of (a) the three genres (STR = storytelling, NWS = newsreading, POR = poetry reciting), (b) extraction method, and (c) pause presence.*

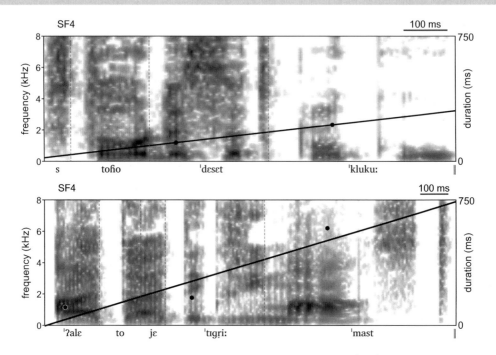

Figure 4.34: *Positive duration slopes, based on extraction in the stressed nuclei (dots), shown as the thick regression line.*

short vowel, but for affective reasons the speaker pronounced it as extremely long, almost 280 ms. In the first example, the slope is 0.30. (Note that we present no units here; it would be possible to express duration slopes in second per second, but this seems somewhat counterintuitive.)

In the next example, we are turning to newsreading, which was mentioned above as displaying a peculiar behaviour of slight acceleration throughout prosodic phrases. Figure 4.35 presents a phrase with a mildly negative duration slope of −0.025, extracted from all syllable nuclei, as a typical phrase demonstrating this trend. As shown in Figure 4.31, negative slopes were more prevalent in internal phrases, and the example provided here is also surrounded by other phrases on both sides.

The last example in Figure 4.36 shows one of the more steeply negative duration gradients – that is, above-average acceleration throughout the phrase. The speaker seems to lengthen the stressed preposition *před*, while the following vowels are progressively shorter, resulting in a rather steep gradient of −0.24. The phrase is internal, but still major (i.e., it is surrounded by other phrases, but ends in a BI4-type of prosodic break); its major character is, in this case, achieved only by melodic means.

Finally, let us turn to speaker-based differences. As can be seen in Figure 4.37, the global trends presented in Figure 4.31 also apply at the individual level; note again that only self-standing phrases are shown. Newsreaders manifest very weak trends, with the duration regression line being nearly straight most of the time. There are only two

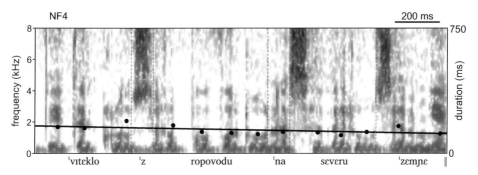

Figure 4.35: *A typical, slightly negative duration slope in newsreading, based on extraction in all syllable nuclei (dots), shown as the thick regression line.*

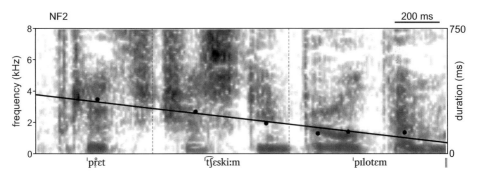

Figure 4.36: *A negative duration slope in newsreading, based on extraction in all syllable nuclei (dots), shown as the thick regression line.*

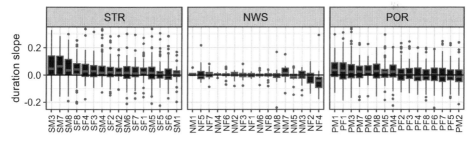

Figure 4.37: *Duration slopes in individual speakers of the three genres (STR = storytelling, NWS = newsreading, POR = poetry reciting), extracted in syllable nuclei.*

newsreaders – NF4 and NF2, whose examples were depicted above in Figs. 4.35 and 4.36 – in whom acceleration prevails. A similar tendency of little changes in syllable duration throughout prosodic phrases is observable in poetry reciting, although there is much greater variability in all speakers. Consequently, what is regarded as a universal tendency of final deceleration (lengthening) is present mostly in our professional actors in storytelling.

4.2.4 VOICE QUALITY

Values of various voice quality parameters were extracted using VoiceSauce (Shue, 2020; Shue et al., 2011). The tool measures a range of parameters which reflect the amount of noise in the spectrum or short-time spectral slope by means of comparing amplitudes of various spectral components (see Hanson & Chuang, 1999, or Tylečková & Skarnitzl, 2019, for more information on these parameters). We used the default settings of VoiceSauce based on Snack f_0 parameter estimation (f_0 detected in the 40–500 Hz range) but with a 5-ms frame shift and with times reported with respect to the centre of the 25-ms analysis window. The resulting contours were again interpolated by a 3-ms step. We only report the results of one parameter here which provides interesting insight, namely cepstral peak prominence, and only when at least two data points (or more exactly, two triplets) are available. Cepstral peak prominence (CPP) is a measure of the amplitude of the cepstral peak which corresponds to f_0, reflecting the harmonic organization of the signal and its amplitude of the signal; it is especially sensitive to breathiness (Hillenbrand, Cleveland & Erickson, 1994; Hejná, Šturm, Tylečková & Bořil, 2021) and hoarseness (Halberstam, 2004).

Boxplots corresponding to CPP slopes in the three genres, extracted using the three approaches above, are shown in Figure 4.38. It should be pointed out that the extraction of CPP is prone to errors and yields many 'undefined' (missing) values. We can see that most slope values are located in the <–5; 5> dB/sec range, more or less centred around zero slope, which is also confirmed in Table 4.8 for most conditions. In some conditions, there is a slight prevalence of positive values; that seems surprising, because positive CPP gradients mean that the amplitude of this major cepstral peak increases slightly between the beginning and end of prosodic phrases, reflecting a 'clearer', more resonant voice. The effect of pause seems to be rather small. CPP slopes manifest a much greater variability in poetry reciting than in the other two genres; this is an artefact of fewer data points after the elimination of phrases containing too many undefined values.

Table 4.8: *Percentage of positive CPP gradients extracted from all points in the three genres (STR = storytelling, NWS = newsreading, POR = poetry reciting), depending on the presence of pauses.*

	Internal	Pre-pausal	Self-standing
STR	56.9	52.2	51.4
NWS	63.5	55.2	54.1
POR	55.6	47.6	50.2

As for the nuclear portions of phrases, Figure 4.39 confirms a trend of positive CPP slopes even here, reflecting lower breathiness or hoarseness within the last stress group. This effect seems to be slightly more prominent in newsreading and poetry re-

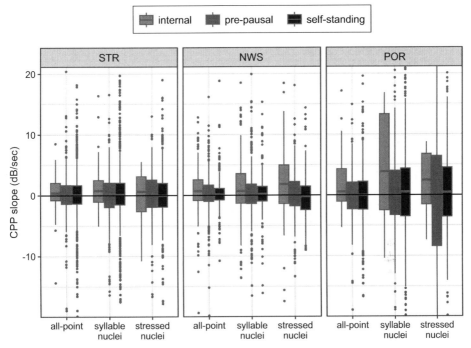

Figure 4.38: *Slopes of cepstral peak prominence (CPP) in the three genres (STR = storytelling, NWS = newsreading, POR = poetry reciting), depending on the presence of pauses, extracted in all points, in all syllable nuclei, and in stressed nuclei only.*

citing than in storytelling. As with intensity in Section 4.2.2 above, a small warning is necessary: the high slope values are not attained in reality, since the duration of the nuclear portions of prosodic phrases is usually well below one second.

LME analysis reveals that the effect of GENRE on CPP slope is not significant ($\chi^2(2)$ = 2.15, p = 0.342); the confidence intervals illustrated in Figure 4.40 are so wide that none of the pairwise comparisons reach significance either. As for the other two fixed factors, the effect of EXTRACTION METHOD turned out to be significant ($\chi^2(3)$ = 285.28, $p < 0.001$); however, it is only the extraction in the nuclear portion of phrases that yields a significantly different CPP slope from all other methods. The effect of PAUSE PRESENCE is also significant ($\chi^2(2)$ = 15.12, $p < 0.001$), with internal phrases manifesting significantly steeper positive slopes than pre-pausal and self-standing phrases.

Finding representative examples of CPP slopes is not easy; as mentioned above, it was by no means rare for the extraction in VoiceSauce to fail. In Figure 4.41, we therefore show a prosodic phrase which manifests a CPP gradient of 0.79 dB/sec, which approaches the mean value, but the empty circles near the bottom of the spectrogram indicate in which syllable nuclei no data points were available (note that we used all-point extraction here).

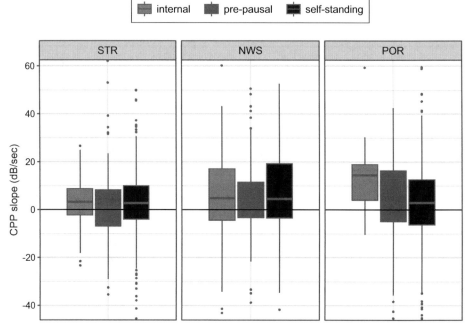

Figure 4.39: *CPP slopes in the three genres (STR = storytelling, NWS = newsreading, POR = poetry reciting), depending on the presence of pauses, extracted in the syllable nuclei of the nuclear portion of each prosodic phrase.*

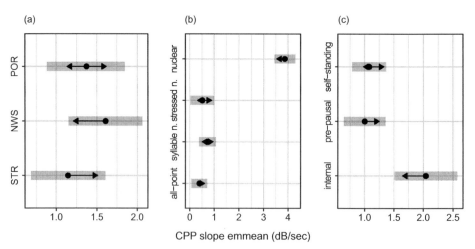

Figure 4.40: *Estimated marginal means of CPP slopes illustrating the effect of (a) the three genres (STR = storytelling, NWS = newsreading, POR = poetry reciting), (b) extraction method, and (c) pause presence.*

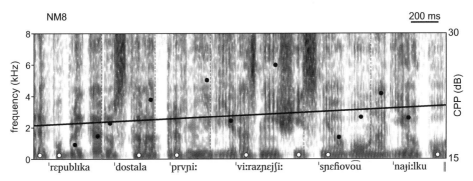

Figure 4.41: *A typical, slightly positive CPP slope, based on extraction in all points, shown as the thick regression line. Values in syllable nuclei are indicated using black dots, missing values in syllable nuclei using empty circles (see text).*

A closer inspection of some of the outlying values of CPP slope revealed that these may often be based on two values of CPP only; such slopes do not really allow for phonetically motivated interpretation. It is worth pointing out that outliers are an inherent part of any analysis but may be better 'concealed' by standard statistical procedures. Still, one more example will be provided: the phrase from poetry reciting in Figure 4.42 shows rather a steep negative CPP slope of −12.53 dB/sec. The empty circles indicate that data are missing for four out of eight syllables, but spectral relations between individual syllables suggest that the resulting slope reasonably reflects reality: while vowel formants are quite well defined in the pronoun *jim*, there is clearly much less energy and more breathiness towards the end of the prosodic phrase.

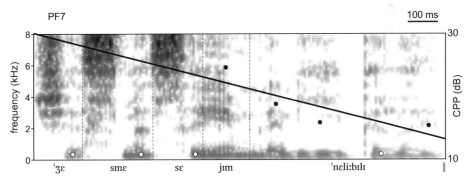

Figure 4.42: *A negative CPP slope, based on extraction in syllable nuclei (black dots), shown as the thick regression line. Missing values in syllable nuclei are indicated using empty circles.*

Finally, the individual speakers' boxplots in Figure 4.43 essentially confirm the global tendencies presented in Figure 4.38. The larger variability in poetry reciting is due to the lower number of valid data points. In the other two genres, most speakers' CPP gradients remain within the <−5; 5> dB/sec range.

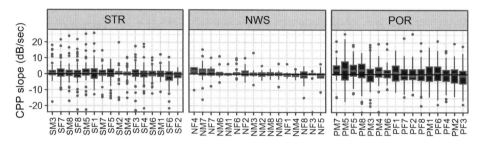

Figure 4.43: *CPP slopes in individual speakers of the three genres (STR = storytelling, NWS = newsreading, POR = poetry reciting), extracted in syllable nuclei.*

4.2.5 DISCUSSION

The aim of section 4.2 was to investigate the acoustic correlates of phrasal structure in Czech, expressed as the slope of acoustic parameters throughout prosodic phrases. All four prosodic domains – melody, dynamics, temporal aspects, and voice quality – were addressed.

From the methodological perspective, we used several manners of data extraction which may be placed on a continuum between ease of application and linguistic interpretability. Extracting parameter values at all points of the signal is on the one hand easy, albeit potentially computationally more demanding, depending on the specific parameter. On the other hand, the extraction of parameter values in syllable nuclei requires the knowledge of boundary placement of individual speech sounds. To be able to do this, all our corpora – 16 speakers in each of the three genres – were manually segmented. Although automatic identification of vocalic sounds in the speech signal is available, these procedures cannot be regarded as completely accurate. For instance, applying the *Extract vowels* script of Praat Vocal Toolkit (Corretge, 2022) on the phrase shown in Figure 4.28 yields only four out of the six vowels. Furthermore, since vowels or syllabic consonants are the carriers of prosodic qualities, using only the information in these sounds is likely to provide information which is more accurate and which better reflects what listeners hear.

In contrast, extracting information from stressed positions is quite restrictive and is not suitable for insufficient data samples. However, the interpretation of the resulting data may be easier; this would be particularly true for languages like English, where the stressed syllable functions as a perceptual anchor and unstressed syllables tend to be reduced. We did not expect the benefit of using only stressed syllables to be large for Czech, a language with very weak, if any, prominence marking on stressed syllables; nevertheless, since the quantity of our data allowed for its testing, this extraction method was also included. Finally, the nuclear portion of prosodic phrases is likely to contain the most salient prosodic information in the entire prosodic phrase; that is why 'zooming in' on the last stress group and examining gradients of prosodic qualities there seemed linguistically sensible provided that enough data was available.

The results of the analyses presented above confirmed that, indeed, the prosodic phrase is a domain within which acoustic parameters change in interpretable ways. Many of the results were not surprising given the abundant literature on prosodic patterns in various languages. For example, negative trends of fundamental frequency have been documented in countless studies, including on Czech (Volín, 2009). Intensity downtrends are also widely attested. It is interesting to examine the relationship between f_0 and intensity downtrends: do speakers who manifest the steepest melodic downtrends behave similarly in the dynamic domain, or are these two dimensions unrelated? In fact, can any correlations be found between slopes in all four dimensions analyzed here?

Table 4.9 presents a correlation matrix of the prosodic dimensions, with data extracted in syllable nuclei of each phrase as input, and irrespective of the three genres. It is clear that when considered from the perspective of prosodic phrases, only the first two dimensions, melodic and dynamic patterning, manifest any interesting degree of relationship between each other, although a correlation coefficient of 0.384 still corresponds to a rather weak link. Correlation matrices were also produced separately for each of the genres, but these provided very little additional information.

Table 4.9: *Correlation matrix of the four slope measures.*

	Intensity slope	f_0 slope	Duration slope
f_0 slope	0.384		
duration slope	−0.049	−0.025	
CPP slope	0.110	0.041	0.044

In Table 4.9, we considered the relationship of two slope values in each prosodic phrase. What we want to focus on is the level of individual speakers. This could be achieved by comparing figures 4.21 and 4.30, but that does not reveal any clear relationship. Let us therefore provide another perspective. Figure 4.44 shows a scatterplot with per-speaker mean values of f_0 and intensity slope. It turns out that the most transparent division concerns the three genres. The figure shows that all the newsreaders (code names starting with N, shown as circles) cluster in the top right corner, with shallowest slopes of both f_0 and intensity. The professional actors in storytelling (code names starting in S, shown as asterisks) and students reciting poetry (code names starting in P, shown as squares) are not as clearly separated, but most speakers in poetry reciting manifest the steepest slopes in both f_0 and intensity, and most storytellers are located in the centre of the plot.

To conclude, Figure 4.45 provides a global summary of the major trends reported in this section. We have confirmed that examining various genres, or potentially speaking styles is a worthwhile effort, since speakers do seem to display genre-specific behaviours. These can be observed particularly in the melodic and dynamic domain

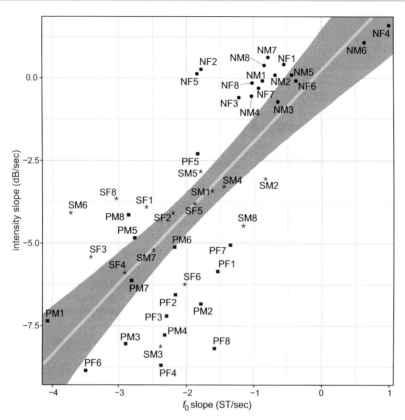

Figure 4.44: *Correlation of mean f_0 and intensity slope in individual speakers of the three genres (asterisks for storytelling, circles for newsreading, squares for poetry reciting). Regression line shown in light grey, confidence interval in dark grey.*

in our data, where newsreading seems to differ from the other two genres. As was already discussed above, differences in the latter domain are likely to be caused by dynamic compression in radio-broadcasted speech. However, the shallower f_0 slopes (see also Figure 4.15) cannot be explained by such processes and are most likely the result of specific speech patterns required of and acquired by the newsreaders. Although the mean values in the temporal domain are all very close to zero, the more detailed perspectives provided in Figures 4.31 and 4.37 show some deceleration (or lengthening) effects in storytelling and almost none in newsreading and poetry reciting, presumably due to the requirement of overall fast speech in the former genre and rhythmic regularity in the latter. The analysis of voice quality was the most problematic part because of missing data; the global means of CPP gradients confirm the somewhat surprising trend of decreasing breathiness or hoarseness throughout phrases in all three genres.

One of the objectives of Section 4.2 was also to illustrate the importance of examining individual cases. Apart from visualizing the typical behaviour of prosodic slopes,

	STR	NWS	POR
f_0 slope	↘ −2.2 ST/sec	→ −0.7 ST/sec	↘ −2.4 ST/sec
intensity slope	↘ −4.6 dB/sec	→ 0.16 dB/sec	↘ −6.5 dB/sec
duration slope	→ 0.04	→ −0.01	→ 0.01
CPP slope	→ 0.3 dB/sec	→ 0.6 dB/sec	→ 0.7 dB/sec

Figure 4.45: *Major trends and mean values of f_0, intensity, duration, and CPP slope in the three genres (STR = storytelling, NWS = newsreading, POR = poetry reciting), extracted in syllable nuclei.*

we exemplified some of the less usual items which were interesting from the viewpoint of specific linguistic or phonetic characteristics, or from the viewpoint of one of the extraction methods. Put simply, many noteworthy things are happening when we take a glimpse beyond averaged behaviours.

4.3 PROSODIC PHRASE SYNTACTICALLY

4.3.1 THEORETICAL UNDERPINNING

The idea that prosody has to 'map' onto syntax is a persistent one. Given the nature of European and American linguistic tradition, its sources are quite clear. Even the elementary formal education in Czech schools seeds syntax into pupils' heads, pretending that it is the cornerstone of understanding the language. As a consequence, there are linguists who believe in the syntax-prosody bond so strongly that they would rather deem their results inexplicable than, for instance, look into semantics (e.g., Clifton, Carson & Frazier, 2002: 104). They may go even further and place syntax above prosody. The wording of "*Presumably, a listener using a grammar of this sort must determine what the prosodic constituency of a sentence implies about its syntactic description*" suggests exactly that (e.g., Clifton, Carson & Frazier, 2002: 106). The idea that a listener will not understand what is said unless he/she analyzes the syntactic structure is one of the common fallacies in linguistics. We believe that the way these views can be reconciled with a beneficial idea of *speaking for the meaning* is to see syntax as an abstract (or distant) reflection of sentence semantics. That is close to Kohler's assertion that syntactic structure serves communicative function in parallel with prosody (2018: 166). A similar claim was voiced by Auer (1996), who supported it with evidence from conversational speech.

Wells (2006: 187) reasserts several times that prosodic phrasing reflects syntactic structure of sentences but does not state how broadly or narrowly he defines syntax.

Nespor and Vogel are more specific and they even admit that syntax does not surface in prosody, but "the construction of prosodic constituents depends on syntactic structure" (1983: 133). In other words, they already see that the idea of direct mapping of syntax onto prosody is untenable, but they do not seem to find the courage to abandon it. They still keep it as the invisible, covert power that makes prosody happen. That manoeuvres them into "restructuring rules" (ibid. pp. 126, 127). One wonders if there would be any need for restructuring if we accepted the natural meaning-oriented basis of phrasing. For that to happen, however, we should not consider style, perception, or cognition as extralinguistic phenomena (*cf.* Nespor & Vogel, 1983: 133).

Our take on the syntax-prosody relationship in this book resonates with Auer's suggestion that prosody and syntax either work hand in hand or split their roles, depending on the momentary requirements of the communicative situation (Auer, 1996). Hence, the key question addressed in this section can be stipulated as follows: How often is the informational and structural setting (in the widest sense) such that a syntactic boundary between subject and predicate of a sentence coincides with a prosodic boundary?

4.3.2 SENTENCE

In this section, the structure of sentences will be examined in a similar manner to that presented for prosodic phrases in Section 4.1. Figure 4.46 displays the length of sentences in the three genres, expressed in the number of prosodic phrases and words; note that the highest length values are pooled. It is interesting to compare storytelling and poetry reciting on the one hand with newsreading on the other: grammatical sentences comprising one or two prosodic phrases are by far the most frequent in the first two genres, but sentences with three phrases prevail in newsreading. Similarly,

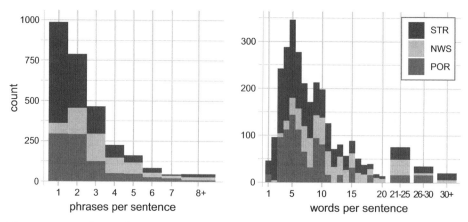

Figure 4.46: *Distribution of various sentence lengths expressed in prosodic phrases and words in three genres (STR = storytelling, NWS = newsreading, POR = poetry reciting).*

sentences with four or more phrases are much more prevalent in newsreading, with 36.6% of all instances; such long sentences (from the perspective of the number of phrases they contain) occur much less frequently in storytelling (13.8%) or poetry reciting (17.8%). The situation is less straightforward when sentence length is expressed in words, as can be seen on the right of Figure 4.46, but the tendency for longer sentences in newsreading is confirmed as well: 76% and 87% of sentences contain ten or fewer words in storytelling and poetry reciting, respectively, while this is only the case in 53% of sentences in newsreading.

To examine the effect of genre on sentence length, we constructed generalized linear mixed-effects (GLME) models with Poisson regression (see Section 4.1 for a more detailed explanation), with Genre defined as a fixed factor and Speaker intercept as a random factor. The effect of Genre is confirmed as significant for prosodic phrases as the dependent variable ($\chi^2(2)$ = 35.28, $p < 0.0001$) as well as words ($\chi^2(2)$ = 33.69, $p < 0.0001$). The effect plots are depicted in Figure 4.47; as in Section 4.1, length is expressed logarithmically, and absolute lengths are provided at the top in grey for easier interpretation. The confidence intervals confirm that sentence length is similar in storytelling and poetry reciting, since their corresponding arrows do not overlap. Sentences are significantly longer in newsreading than in the other genres.

It is worth considering not only the length of grammatical sentences, as expressed in linguistic units, but also their absolute duration. It is not surprising that, as shown in Figure 4.48, the overall tendencies observed for sentence length in phrases and words hold also for duration in seconds. Sentences in newsreading are markedly longer, as shown by the Q3–Q1 boxes. In fact, mean duration is nearly identical for storytelling and poetry reciting (3.125 seconds and 3.093 seconds, respectively), whereas in newsreading it is higher by more than one second (4.372 seconds). What is more interesting, however, are the outliers depicted as dark dots. One can see that sentences longer than 15 seconds only occur in storytelling.

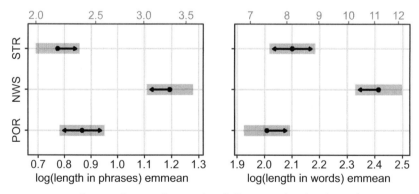

Figure 4.47: *Estimated marginal means of sentence length illustrating the effect of genre (STR = storytelling, NWS = newsreading, POR = poetry reciting). Sentence length is expressed in prosodic phrases (left) and words (right), as a logarithm (absolute lengths are shown in grey at the top). Bars correspond to confidence intervals of the emmeans, and arrows serve for comparisons between them (see text).*

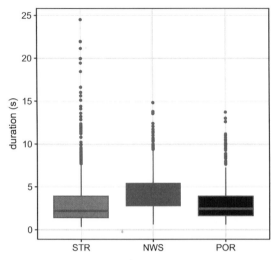

Figure 4.48: *Sentence duration in the three genres (STR = storytelling, NWS = newsreading, POR = poetry reciting).*

A closer examination of these eleven very long sentences in storytelling reveals that seven of them were produced by a single speaker, SM2, and that this has more to do with the text read by the actor (a story by the Czech author Jaroslav Hašek from 1923) than with the actor's idiosyncratic language use. The longest sentence – which comprises 16 prosodic phrases and 46 words and its duration is 23.832 seconds – is provided in example (17). Prosodic phrase boundaries, as realized by the actor, are indicated using the corresponding symbols: ‖ for the major, BI4-type break and | for the minor, BI3-type break.

(17) Nepřestal jsem si vážiti poštovní instituce ‖ která prodělala od dob Marie Terezie | celou řadu různých změn ‖ od trestání postilionů na hrdle ‖ za ztrátu zapečetěného psaní ‖ až | po zavedení dopisnic | a pohlednic ‖ od zrušení poštovních stanic ‖ nešťastnými omnibusovými kočáry ‖ až | po zavedení poštovních ambulancí ve vlaku ‖

I have not lost my appreciation for the postal institution ‖ which has undergone since the days of Maria Theresa | a variety of changes ‖ from the punishment of postilions by losing their head ‖ for the loss of sealed writing ‖ to | the introduction of letters | and postcards ‖ from the abolition of post offices ‖ by the ill-fated omnibus coaches ‖ to | the introduction of postal ambulances on the train ‖

The example (albeit extreme) indicates that a lot of individual speaker variability is concealed in the data presented so far. Sentence length per speaker is illustrated in Figure 4.49. One can immediately see the strong similarities between speakers in poetry reciting. Between 60 and 75% of all sentences in poetry reciters comprise a maximum of two prosodic phrases. Sentences of one or two prosodic phrases are also prevalent in storytelling, accounting for slightly below 50% only in speakers SF5 and SM2 and between 55% and 92% in all the others. As was already mentioned, speaker SM2,

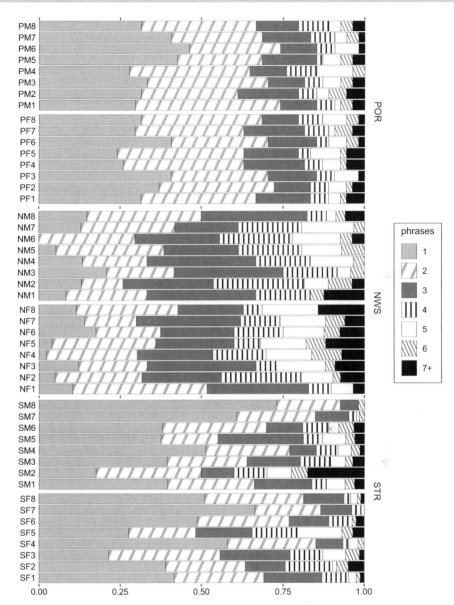

Figure 4.49: *Sentence length in individual speakers of the three genres (STR = storytelling, NWS = newsreading, POR = poetry reciting), expressed in prosodic phrases (shortest sentences on the left, longest on the right).*

whose example was mentioned above, is exceptional in the number of sentences which contain seven or more prosodic phrases: this happened in seven out of the 40 analyzed sentences (that is, in 17.5%). Turning to newsreading, it is obvious that the overall tendency to create longer sentences in this genre is confirmed also at the individual level, with only speakers NF1 and NM8 having 50% or more sentences composed of no more than one or two phrases. For six out of the 16 speakers, sentences with three prosodic phrases were the most frequent, and for one (NM2) it was sentences with three and four phrases (15 occurrences of each). Interestingly, speaker NM6 did not produce a single sentence which would correspond only to one prosodic phrase. Finally, it is also interesting to note that long sentences of seven or more phrases occurred much more frequently in our female newsreaders.

From the viewpoint of individual variability, it is evident that poetry reciting imposes the strictest limits on how sentences may be structured internally. That is to be expected, of course, given the fact that all of our speakers performed the same poems. Figure 4.49 showed that individual variability is much greater in storytelling than in poetry reciting; it is probable that this largely reflects the writing style of the respective authors, as was the case with example (17) above. Finally, our newsreaders lie between the actors in storytelling and students reciting poetry in terms of idiosyncratic behaviour: the newsreading genre also does impose some restrictions on the structure of the texts. On the one hand, the content of news is rarely communicated using very short sentences; on the other hand, however, the requirement of clarity prevents speakers from long, convoluted sentences such as those observed in some storytellers.

4.3.3 SUBJECT-PREDICATE BOUNDARY

From the vast area of syntactic phenomena, we investigated the boundary between the subject (Sub) and predicate (Pre) constituents. These two constituents represent the coarsest division of a typical sentence. In other words, the subject-predicate structure is to be expected in most sentences generated in language communication, while the more refined classification of sentence constituents can happen in reference to the subject or predicate part. The subject is generally something or someone that the sentence is about, while the predicate ascribes the subject some quality, state, action, etc. One of the reasons why the syntactic boundary between the subject and predicate attracted our attention is the fact that older written texts in Czech used to signal it with a comma, while current orthographic rules do not permit any punctuation between the subject and predicate (*cf.* Grepl & Karlík, 1986: 22). The chief objective of this section is to find out how frequently a prosodic boundary coincides with the syntactic subject-predicate division.

EXPLICIT VS. IMPLICIT SUBJECT

The material (as described in Chapter 3) provided 2,805 sentences. However, we were only interested in sentences where the syntactic subject is explicit, i.e., expressed by a word actually present in the text. Given our research question, sentences with im-

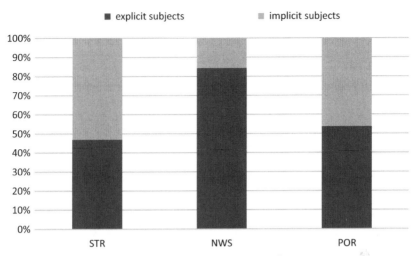

Figure 4.50: *Ratios of explicit and implicit subjects in the three genres (STR = storytelling, NWS = newsreading, POR = poetry reciting).*

plicit or null subjects could not be considered. Figure 4.50 displays the ratios of explicit subjects in our material broken by the genre.

There is a visible difference between newsreading and the other two genres. Clearly, the news bulletins favour explicitly stated subjects of their sentences. In stories, slightly more than a half (52.5%) of the syntactic subjects have to be understood from the context. Similarly, in our sample of poems, almost a half of the subjects were implicit (46.3%). In the news reports, 84.3% of the syntactic subjects were explicit.

SUBJECT LENGTH (IN WORDS)

The explicit subject is usually expressed with a noun or pronoun, but the cases where an infinitive serves as a subject are not rare either (e.g., *Zahodit takovou příležitost by bylo hloupé/ To waste such an opportunity would be silly*). Similarly, a dependent subject clause is a possibility (e.g., *Je zcela pochopitelné, že takový člověk byl všude vítán/ It is quite understandable that a person of his qualities was appreciated everywhere*).

Even if a noun is the core of the subject, it can be expanded with various attributes into a noun phrase. Therefore, we were interested in how long (expressed in words) the subjects typically were. In the storytelling material, the mean extent of a subject was 3.1 words. However, the rightmost column in Table 4.10 reveals substantial individual differences. Whereas the text produced by speaker SM8 had subjects that were on average 1.3 word long, the mean size of the subject produced by speaker SF5 was 5.6 words. It is worth comparing these values with overall sentence length, as presented in Section 4.3.2 and Figure 4.49: speaker SM8 can be seen to have the shortest and speaker SF5 the longest sentences (expressed in the number of prosodic phrases).

Table 4.10 also displays information about the count of explicit subjects in individual subsamples and the ratio (or rather percentage) of one-word subjects in the given set. Unsurprisingly, there is a negative correlation between mean subject length and the proportion of one-word subjects. This means that the greater the representation of one-word subjects in the set, the smaller the mean size of the subject. Pearson correlation coefficient for this relationship was $r = -0.85$, which means a high association of the two measures.

Table 4.10: *Descriptors of syntactic subjects produced by individual speakers in the storytelling material (STR).*

Speaker	Number of explicit subjects	Number of one-word subjects	Ratio of one-word subjects (%)	Subject length (words)
SF1	42	23	54.8	2.1
SF2	31	20	64.5	1.8
SF3	37	15	40.5	3.5
SF4	49	31	63.3	2.0
SF5	23	8	34.8	5.6
SF6	28	15	53.6	2.7
SF7	30	23	76.7	1.6
SF8	51	24	47.1	3.0
SM1	31	9	29.0	4.9
SM2	29	12	41.4	5.1
SM3	37	17	45.9	4.5
SM4	37	19	51.4	2.5
SM5	29	8	27.6	4.2
SM6	31	20	64.5	3.1
SM7	71	42	59.2	1.8
SM8	62	51	82.3	1.3

Table 4.11 displays information concerning subject length in the newsreading material. The mean for the whole sample is 3.3 words, which is slightly more than in storytelling (above). This difference is statistically insignificant, but what is noteworthy is the substantial difference in the homogeneity of means. In the narratives the mean length varied between 1.3 and 5.6 words, while in the news bulletins it was only between 2.7 and 4.3. This again parallels to some extent the overall homogeneity of sentence length (*cf.* Figure 4.48).

Table 4.11: *Descriptors of syntactic subjects produced by individual speakers in the newsreading material (NWS).*

Speaker	Number of explicit subjects	Number of one-word subjects	Ratio of one-word subjects (%)	Subject length (words)
NF1	26	8	30.8	3.2
NF2	33	6	18.2	3.1
NF3	29	11	37.9	3.3
NF4	34	9	26.5	3.4
NF5	41	16	39.0	3.8
NF6	35	9	25.7	4.3
NF7	42	13	31.0	3.2
NF8	30	6	20.0	3.0
NM1	22	2	9.1	2.9
NM2	38	7	18.4	3.6
NM3	39	9	23.1	2.9
NM4	23	6	26.1	3.4
NM5	51	12	23.5	3.2
NM6	25	4	16.0	3.3
NM7	27	10	37.0	3.4
NM8	31	12	38.7	2.7

The table also shows that the proportion of one-word subjects is much lower in news reports. Whereas narratives contained 52% of such subjects, in the NWS material it was merely a half of that, 26%. Moreover, the correlation between mean subject length and the proportion of one-word subjects was very low and statistically insignificant, clearly due to small variation in mean lengths of subjects.

Table 4.12: *Descriptors of syntactic subjects produced in the poems (POR): n SubExp = number of explicit subjects.*

Speaker	Number of explicit subjects	Number of one-word subjects	Ratio of one-word subjects (%)	Subject length (words)
All	28	18	62.1	1.8

The texts in poetry reciting (POR) did not vary. Therefore, the table analogous to Tables 4.10 and 4.11 has only one set of descriptors for all speakers (Tab. 4.12). It is evident that mean subject length is much lower than in the previous two genres. The proportion of one-word subjects is, however, quite high. These uniform descriptors are nevertheless still important, since our research question concerned the coincidence of prosodic breaks and the subject-predicate boundaries. In other words, if the syntax is uniform, will the prosodic marking of the subject-predicate division also be uniform? The answer is provided in the following subsection.

PHRASAL BREAK AT THE SUBJECT-PREDICATE BOUNDARY

When presenting the coincidence of subject delineation and prosodic boundaries, one has to remember that the predicate can either follow (Sub-Pre) or precede (Pre-Sub). In some cases, the predicate can enclose the subject (Pre-Sub-Pre), i.e., precede and follow by its two parts. (The cases of split subject, however, occurred in less than 0.1% cases.) Although Czech is reported as an SVO language, Figure 4.51 shows that there was a non-negligible number of predicates preceding the subject. In fact, the number of Sub-Pre orderings is about the same as the sum of Pre-Sub and Pre-Sub-Pre orderings.

The mutual ratios of the orderings in the three genres are displayed in Figure 4.52. They are not monotonous: the largest number of instances of the unmarked Sub-Pre order was found in narratives (STR), but the news bulletins (NWS) were quite similar

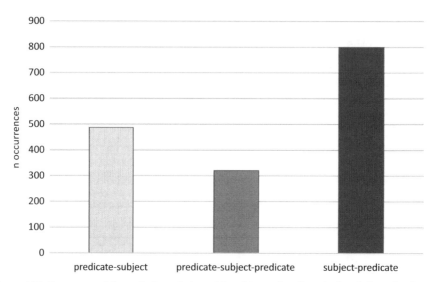

Figure 4.51: *Occurrences of three relative orderings of the subject and predicate in the whole analyzed material. Pre-Sub = predicate-subject order; Pre-Sub-Pre = subject preceded and followed by parts of the predicate; Sub-Pre = subject-predicate order.*

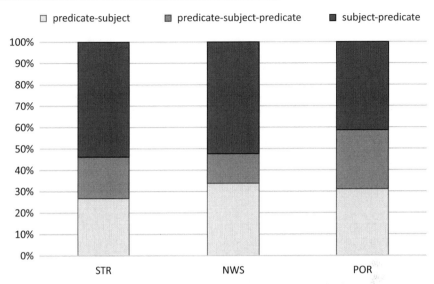

Figure 4.52: *Ratios of three ascertained orderings of subjects and predicates in the three genres (STR = storytelling, NWS = newsreading, POR = poetry reciting). Pre-Sub = predicate-subject order; Pre-Sub-Pre = subject preceded and followed by parts of the predicate; Sub-Pre = subject-predicate order.*

in this sense. The difference between these two genres lied in a much lower occurrence of split predicates (Pre-Sub-Pre) in news, hence the higher number of simple Pre-Sub cases there. Poetry reciting (POR) had the highest relative occurrence of Pre-Sub-Pre instances, and it was at the expense of the unmarked Sub-Pre orderings. As acknowledged above, however, the sample of POR was not suitable for genre analysis focused on textual properties. It was prepared for the speech production analysis – specifically for observation of prosodic phrase boundaries in identical texts.

Altogether, 1,928 boundaries between explicit subject and predicate were identified in the material (808 in a transition from predicate to subject, 1,120 in a transition from subject to predicate). Coincidence with a prosodic phrase boundary at these transitions was found in 627 cases. In other words, 32.5% of syntactic boundaries between the subject and predicate constituents concurred with prosodic boundaries. From the opposite perspective, about two thirds of syntactic dividing lines between subject and predicate of a sentence were not accompanied by phrasal boundaries.

Individual genres, however, contributed to this overall result quite differently. The highest coincidence of syntactic and prosodic boundaries was found in newsreading: 46.6%. The lowest, on the other hand, was found in storytelling: 22.8%. Poetry reciting was in between: 30.4%.

Two potential factors for coincidence were tested: first, the ordering of constituents, and second, the length of the subject. Table 4.13 shows what percentage of all subject-predicate transitions coincided with prosodic phrase boundaries under the Pre-Sub and Sub-Pre conditions. (Pre-Sub-Pre cases contain both types of transition and, therefore, informed both columns.)

Table 4.13: *Percentages of phrasal boundaries coinciding with syntactic boundaries for two different orderings: predicate-subject and subject-predicate.*

Genre	Coincidence in predicate-subject (%)	Coincidence in subject-predicate (%)
STR	14.7	27.9
NWS	33.9	55.7
POR	40.1	22.2
All	29.2	34.9

Both in storytelling and newsreading, the opportunities for a syntax-prosody match were exploited much more often in the unmarked Sub-Pre transition. In storytelling, it was almost twice as often. In poetry reciting, the trend was contrary to the previous one, but it has to be remembered that this sample is textually not as representative as the other two samples. Be that as it may, if we disregard the genre, the occurrence of a syntax-prosody match was higher in the Sub-Pre transition than in the Pre-Sub one (34.9% and 29.2%, respectively). In other words, if the predicate precedes the subject, it is less probable that the prosodic break will follow after it.

The length of the subject also proved to play a role. Quite unsurprisingly, the longer the subject, the greater the chance that it will be separated from the predicate by a prosodic boundary. The quantification of this effect in our sample is shown in Table 4.14.

Table 4.14: *Percentages of phrasal boundaries coinciding with syntactic boundaries for various lengths of the sentence subject: one-word, two-word, three-word, and four-word or longer subjects.*

Genre	1-word (%)	2-word (%)	3-word (%)	4+word (%)
STR	11.6	31.0	30.0	51.6
NWS	27.2	52.0	60.0	58.3
POR	23.9	29.2	68.8	46.9
All	24.3	37.8	52.7	54.8

The last summarizing line of Table 4.14 shows that when all the speech material was pooled together, one-word subjects were separated from their predicates with a prosodic boundary in about one quarter of the cases. Subjects of two-word length were separated from their predicates in more than one third of the cases. Three-word subjects exploited more than a half of their predicate transitions to be marked with a prosodic break, and subjects of four or more words did not change the picture much.

However, considerable differences can be seen across the individual genres. In storytelling, the speakers were quite reluctant to separate one-word subjects from their predicates: only 11.6% of the syntactic boundaries of this sort were matched with phrasal breaks. A lexico-semantic analysis in the future might bring insight into this result.

DISCUSSION

Due to its rich inflectional system, the Czech language does not require the syntactic subject to be explicitly represented in a sentence. In fact, in 38% of our almost 3,000 sentences, the subject was only implicit. Interestingly, a much lower ratio of implicit subjects was found in newsreading (only about 15%): news bulletins obviously require explicit representation of sentence subjects more than the other two genres, which might be caused by the higher information density and relatively rapid change of topics.

In the rest of the sentences, the explicit representation of the sentence subject allowed for a certain question to be asked. A preliminary one concerned the length of the subject. In this respect, poetry differed from the other two genres in that there was a high incidence of one-word subjects and the mean length of the subject was therefore much lower (not even two words). Both news reports and narratives had the mean length of the subject slightly over three words, but they still differed mutually in that the variation in length was much lower in the former than in the latter. Again, we could explain this tentatively by hypothesizing that news bulletins represent a more template-like forms, while narratives are much less restricted in the forms that build them.

The core question of this section was that of coincidences between phrasal breaks and subject-predicate boundaries. We found that nearly a third of all transitions between the subject and predicate in a sentence concurred with phrasal breaks. The occurrence of such matches between prosody and syntax was influenced by the length of the subject, but also by the mutual position (ordering) of the two constituents. The unmarked ordering (with the predicate following the subject) was relatively more often hosting a prosodic break.

One of the tasks for future research is to investigate the behaviour of other syntactic constituents. We believe that sentences with adverbials in initial position are good candidates for the next step – they also present the situation in which prosody and syntax work hand in hand. The question is to what extent and under what further circumstances.

However, as stated several times in this book, there should be a growing awareness of the fact that it is not syntax that governs prosody, it is wider semantics. When the founder of the Prague Linguistic Circle, Vilém Mathesius, complained that the difference between the grammatical structure of a sentence and its semantic (pragmatic) structure had been ignored in linguistics despite being admitted for decades (Mathesius, 1939: 171), he did not know that this fact would still be true for many decades to come. Nevertheless, in our context it would be interesting to find what the semantic (informational) status of subjects in our material was. In other words, we should investigate how often the syntactic subject is also the theme of the message, or even the core of the theme (theme proper in Firbas' terminology), and what other roles it can play in the information structure. This is a part of our plans for the future.

5.
PROSODIC PHRASE PERCEPTUALLY

Previous research has identified recurring acoustic attributes associated with phrasing (see Sections 2.3 and especially 4.2). On the one hand, these encompass the presence of local features that are emblematic of prosodic boundaries, such as the presence of pauses, voice quality phenomena like breathiness, creakiness or nasality, final deceleration (frequently referred to as lengthening; see Section 1.3), or nuclear melodic configurations. On the other hand, features distributed throughout the prosodic phrase globally, such as declination in f0, intensity, and tempo, are involved in indicating phrase length and projecting closure.

Besides measuring acoustic correlates of phrasing and prosodic breaks, it is crucial to ascertain which of these markers of prosodic phrasing hold perceptual significance for listeners. Such an analysis would need to extend to diverse languages, not only Czech, given the indications that differential cue weighting may occur in languages (see Sections 5.1 and 5.2). Furthermore, considering the availability of phonetic form, a fundamental question arises as to the purpose prosodic phrasing serves. In Section 5.3, we provide an overview of the possible functions of prosodic phrasing and expand on it in Section 5.4 by presenting an experiment centred on memory recall in Czech.

5.1 PERCEPTUAL CUES TO PROSODIC PHRASING

Among the numerous acoustic cues to prosodic phrasing listed in the introduction to this section, only few have been examined from the perceptual point of view. The challenge lies in untangling the influence of individual cues, given that human perception operates holistically, making use of redundancy and compensation mechanisms (Remez, 2021). Furthermore, the perceptual process involves the integration of the prosodic cues with lexico-syntactic and pragmatic information, among other factors (*cf.* Section 4.3). Effectively, listeners rely on this comprehensive array of features to anticipate forthcoming prosodic boundaries and to interpret the structure of utterances. Fully exploring and evaluating the interaction of the contributing factors is therefore an arduous task which, of course, cannot be resolved within the scope of this book.

A prominent role in these efforts belongs to pauses, which have been extensively studied both in production (e.g., Zellner, 1994; Campione & Véronis, 2002; Werner, Trouvain & Möbius, 2022; Šturm & Volín, 2023) and in perception (e.g., Carlson et al. 2005; Lin & Fon, 2009; Männel and Friederici 2016; Price, 2021; Volín & Šturm, 2023). Although pauses seem intuitively crucial for phrasing, they often display considerable variability across speakers, genres, styles, or speaking tasks, and they have even been found to be optional. Nevertheless, experimental evidence supports the notion that pauses, when present, serve as robust cues for prosodic boundary perception. For instance, researchers have manipulated the acoustic signal by altering pause duration or removing pauses from the spoken material, frequently employing highly artificial sentences such as "A and B or C." As an example, Scott (1982) found that listeners effectively grouped B with A or C when a longer pause was present between the two items, with their performance further improved when both a pause and final deceleration were included.

It is always crucial to consider the methodological context of the studies. Different conclusions can be reached depending on the type of speech (natural vs. synthesized, etc.) or on the duration of the pauses used. In contrast to Scott (1982), the pause was not found to be a sufficient cue for eliciting a change in the grouping in the study of Aasland and Baum (2003), while manipulating the degree of final deceleration did shift the boundary perception. The most pronounced effect was present when both cues – pauses and final deceleration – co-occurred. The methodological caveat lies in the fact that the impact of pauses observed in their study (or also in Zhang, 2012) might have been underestimated because relatively short pause durations were used (maximally 80 ms or 160 ms, respectively), whereas spontaneous speech or the material in other studies typically feature longer pauses. Interestingly, despite this short duration of pauses, Zhang's (2012) study demonstrated a language-dependent perceptual significance of the three analyzed cues (pause, final deceleration, and f_0 reset). Specifically, while final deceleration was the least effective for both English and Mandarin Chinese listeners, pauses carried greater weight for the former and f_0 reset for the latter group. In a study by Jeon and Nolan (2013), Korean participants exhibited a similar pattern to Zhang's English participants when identifying prosodic phrases within digit sequences. They located the boundary either early or late in the sequence relying more on temporal cues (final deceleration) than on f_0 cues. Multiple lines of research into German (e.g., Männel & Friederici, 2016; Petrone et al., 2017) have also consistently emphasized the prominence of temporal cues over melodic cues.

Examining the role of individual cues in prosodic boundary perception, the study of Lin and Fon (2009) showed how their utilization varies depending on the specific experimental task at hand. A random set of 18-syllable sequences was concatenated from the syllables [bu], [di], and [ga]. Each sequence was then manipulated under three conditions of final syllable lengthening (no lengthening, 80 ms, 120 ms) and pause duration (no pause, 400 ms, 600 ms). When the task was to detect a prosodic boundary within such a sequence, namely, to press a button as soon as the first "sentence" ended, Lin and Fon observed that greater final deceleration resulted in quicker reactions compared to variations in pause duration. However, when (other) participants were instructed to assess the strength of the perceived boundary using a 5-point scale, pause duration emerged as a more important factor than lengthening of the final syllable. Notably, deceleration exerted a discernible effect only in instances where no pause was present.

The authors concluded that "for listeners, final lengthening is the main cue signalling the end of speech, and pause duration determines boundary strength" (p. 811). Nevertheless, it is worth emphasizing that this conclusion may be somewhat tethered to the specific experimental setup, and caution is necessary when generalizing these findings. Be that as it may, the results demonstrated that prosodic phrasing can be effectively conveyed through durational cues alone (f_0 was consistently set at 210 Hz), underscoring the flexibility of listeners in adapting to different cues within the perceptual process.

Regarding the contribution of individual cues, an important study was conducted by Yang, Shen, Li and Yang (2014). They used Chinese sentences structured around two prosodic phrases, demarcated with a critical boundary. The researchers systematically manipulated boundary cues through acoustic alterations, such as removing the pause, shortening pre-boundary segment durations, and substituting f_0 contours. Participants were tasked with either detecting the presence of a boundary or evaluating its strength on a 7-point scale. The design included several conditions: two baselines, where no or all features were preserved; three conditions preserving only a single feature (pause, final deceleration, or f_0 reset); and one condition preserving two features (pause and final deceleration).

The results showed an interesting outcome. All three parameters were associated with significantly higher rates of detected boundaries compared to the no-cue condition. Notably, the presence of a pause yielded the most substantial increase in detection rates (from 40% in the baseline to approximately 80%), followed by final deceleration and f_0 reset (both at around 60% of detected boundaries). However, there seems to be a ceiling effect, as combining deceleration with a pause or preserving all features did not further enhance the participants' performance. These findings suggest that the pause emerges as the most crucial cue for boundary perception in Mandarin Chinese, while f_0 reset and final deceleration play additional, albeit weaker, roles.

The data obtained from the participants' ratings exhibited a similar pattern. The inclusion of a pause had the most pronounced impact on the perceived strength of the boundary, overshadowing the effects of the other two cues. Again, there was no additional effect when these cues were used in combination. In summary, the research leads to the conclusion that the perception of a prosodic boundary in Chinese heavily hinges on the presence of a pause, to the extent that it may outweigh the contribution of other parameters. Additionally, the authors noted that in contrast to production data, where f_0 reset is reported to be more salient, f_0 reset and final deceleration were perceptually equivalent in their experiment.

In a different approach, Carlson, Hirschberg and Swerts (2005) selected fragments from spontaneous Swedish speech and presented them to both Swedish and

American listeners. Rather than focusing on a boundary between two parts, the task was to judge whether the fragment was terminated with a prosodic boundary and, if detected, evaluate its strength on a 5-point scale. All chosen fragments originally preceded the word *and* in Swedish and were balanced for the presence of a boundary at their conclusion (categorized as either "no boundary", "weak boundary" or "major boundary", as identified by three expert listeners). The experiment aimed at addressing two key questions: firstly, whether pauses were indispensable for identifying prosodic boundaries, and secondly, whether lexico-grammatical factors were necessary for this task.

Given that pauses were intentionally omitted from the stimuli, listeners were required to rely on alternative acoustic cues. The participants' judgments were notably accurate, aligning closely with the boundary labels assigned by the expert listeners. Correlation analyses suggested that listeners primarily depended on the values of f_0 level and slope, as well as the presence of the final creak. It was also observed that final deceleration was more closely associated with minor boundaries than with major ones. Remarkably, both native and non-native listeners demonstrated a high degree of accuracy in identifying the prosodic boundaries. This success among listeners without access to the semantic content of the fragments underscores the significant role of prosody in boundary perception, independent of lexical and grammatical factors.

Finally, the experiment was conducted in two variations: one utilizing complete fragments lasting approximately two seconds, and the other presenting only the final word to the listeners. This approach allowed for an evaluation of the contribution of different parts within the fragments to the decision-making process. Interestingly, while longer stretches did yield more consistent ratings, as anticipated, the disparity in accuracy between the two was relatively modest. This observation indicates that the critical information for boundary perception is primarily concentrated within the final word of the phrase.

5.2 EXPERIMENT ON CUE WEIGHTING IN CZECH

In light of the above findings, we conducted an experiment[1] to investigate the perception of prosodic boundaries in the Czech language. It was inspired by the methodology employed in Yang et al. (2014), although our approach featured several modifications. Our primary goal was to assess the influence of two distinct durational cues: *presence of a pause* and *final deceleration*. To mitigate any potential influence of melodic cues on our results, we resynthesized all audio files with a monotonous f_0 contour (*cf.* Lin & Fon, 2009).

---

[1] The research was conducted as part of the Speech Perception Research Seminar at Charles University in 2022/23. Students prepared the material and administered the test under the supervision of the instructor, Pavel Šturm. Their contribution is thus acknowledged.

5.2.1 MATERIAL AND METHODS

The experiment involved four distinct conditions (Table 5.1). Our prediction was that retaining the individual cues (conditions B, C) within the stimuli would increase the ratings of boundary judgment compared to the baseline condition A, where all the considered boundary features were either eliminated or neutralized. Condition D, which combined two features concurrently, was predicted to yield the highest boundary strength ratings. Based on the findings presented above, however, it is also possible for the combination of features in condition D not to increase boundary strength perception as compared to condition C. In the absence of any influence from these parameters on boundary perception in Czech, we would expect no discernible differences across the various conditions.

Table 5.1: *Experimental conditions and the phonetic features that were retained versus manipulated.*

Condition	Features retained	Features removed/changed
A (= baseline)	—	f_0, pause, deceleration
B	deceleration	f_0, pause
C	pause	f_0, deceleration
D	pause, deceleration	f_0

The manipulations were carried out in Praat. For the pause manipulation, we employed a straightforward approach of trimming pauses at zero crossings in the sound editor. To address the f_0 manipulation, adjustments were made within the PSOLA Manipulation window, where all f_0 points were set to the 25th percentile of the original f_0 contour. Furthermore, final deceleration was eliminated through PSOLA as well. In this process, the duration of the final syllable rime, encompassing the vowel nucleus and coda if present, was set to a fixed value of 0.6, corresponding to 60% of the original duration and effectively resulting in a shortening of 40%. This specific manipulation was inspired by the work of Volín and Skarnitzl (2007), which identified temporal downtrends in Czech read speech. Subsequently, all stimuli were saved as new audio files.

The recordings for the experiment were taken from our storytelling corpus (that is, the audiobook narratives described in Chapter 3). Three female and three male speakers were chosen. Each target item was composed of two major prosodic phrases, separated by a prosodic break located in the middle third of the item (e.g., *téměř nemožným ‖ skutečně ho navštívit*, which translates to *almost impossible ‖ to actually visit him* in English). The fragments did not necessarily form complete sentences, as the initial and especially final words in the sentence were usually omitted (also due to frequent occurrence of creaky phonation where PSOLA manipulations are known to fail). Apart from the target prosodic break in the middle, there were no other discernible prosodic breaks, except for the possible final one occurring after the last word. Additionally, filler items were provided, designed as distractors for the participants. They either featured a very clear prosodic boundary in the middle or lacked any boundaries throughout the item. The aim of including filler items was to conceal the acoustic manipulations and to provide a broader spectrum for the rating process.

A total of 32 native Czech listeners took part in the experiment (6 males, 26 females, with an average age of 23.8 years). Their task was to assess the degree of auditory coherence between two segments of a sentence. The participants were presented with the text of the two segments, visually separated by a small gap, as illustrated in Figure 5.1. Subsequently, the audio playback started automatically after a 2-second delay, with the option for one replay if needed. The listeners then indicated their assessment on a continuous scale ranging from "very tightly" (connected by their sound) on the left to "very loosely" on the right using a movable slider. Higher numbers thus indicate stronger prosodic boundaries. Importantly, the instructions were very clear about the nature of the task, repeatedly emphasizing that the evaluation pertained solely to the auditory aspects and did not encompass considerations related to grammatical relationships between words. The position of the slider was transformed into the numerical scale between 0 (very tightly) and 1 (very loosely).

There were 24 target items, with each speaker contributing four distinct items to the dataset. A corresponding set of 24 filler items was also included. The analysis was thus based on 768 target ratings and 768 filler ratings. The presentation order of all items was randomized for each participant apart from six additional training items

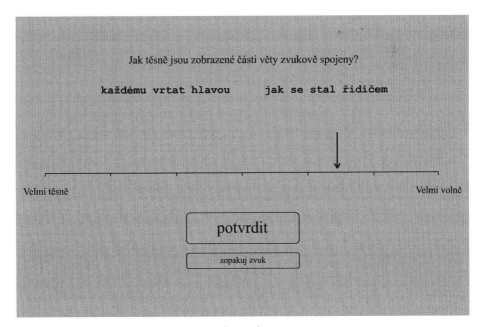

Figure 5.1: *Screenshot of the experimental setup (see text).*

designed for practice and task familiarization. (It is worth noting that these practice items included representations of all conditions and voices, although their content differed from the subsequent target and filler items.) The experiment was conducted individually in the recording studio of the Institute of Phonetics, with each session lasting approximately 12–15 minutes.

To avoid participants having to rate the same textually identical items multiple times due to the four manipulated conditions of the target items, we adopted a counterbalancing approach. The target items were each presented in one condition only, with this distribution balanced across speakers and listeners. As a result, we organized participants into four distinct groups, each consisting of eight listeners. This design ensured that every target item within a given condition was evaluated by the same number of participants, and each listener assessed an equivalent number of target items within a condition.

5.2.2 RESULTS AND DISCUSSION

To verify that participants were effectively evaluating the strength of prosodic boundaries as instructed, we first analyzed the set of filler items with unambiguous properties, as illustrated in the left panel of Figure 5.2. Type 1 fillers, which lacked a prosodic boundary, were indeed rated towards the "tight" end of the scale (mean = 0.13, median = 0.08). Conversely, Type 2 fillers, featuring a clear prosodic boundary, were on average rated toward the opposite end of the scale (mean = 0.69, median = 0.72). None of the listeners exhibited a reversed or neutralized pattern of ratings, confirming their adherence to the experimental instructions.

Additionally, as an interesting side analysis, we examined unrefined engagement times as an indicator of participant uncertainty. The typical engagement time for target items was approximately 5 seconds (SD = 4.1 s). It is notable that there was a negative correlation between trial number and logarithmically expressed engagement time ($r = -0.18$, CI = -0.25 to -0.11, $p < 0.001$), suggesting slightly quicker decision-making as the experiment progressed.

Moving on to the right panel of Figure 5.2, we observe the responses to the target items. Conditions C and D (pause × pause + deceleration) appear not to have been differentiated by the listeners. This highlights the crucial role of the pause, as the shift from A to C/D was more substantial compared to the shift from A to B.

To assess the statistical significance of these findings, we constructed a linear mixed-effects model using the *lme4* package. The random component of the model included a random intercept for each ITEM and both a random intercept and a random slope for each LISTENER. The fixed component included the effect of CONDITION (A, B, C, D). Likelihood ratio tests confirmed a highly significant effect: $\chi^2(3) = 56.8$, $p < 0.001$. Figure 5.3 presents the model's output, illustrating the predicted boundary strength ratings for each condition. All pairwise comparisons between the conditions were found to be statistically significant, except for C vs. D.

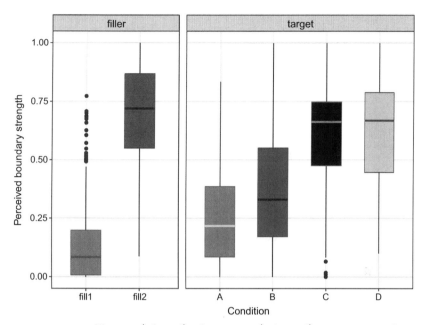

Figure 5.2: *Responses to filler items (left panel) and target items (right panel). A = no cue retained, B = deceleration, C = pause, D = pause + deceleration; 0 = "very tight", 1 = "very loose" connection.*

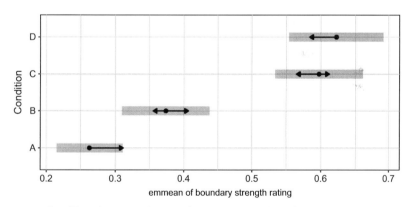

Figure 5.3: *Predicted boundary strength ratings (A = no cue retained, B = deceleration, C = pause, D = pause + deceleration; 0 = "very tight", 1 = "very loose" connection).*

The robustness of the observed effect is evident when examining the consistency across participants. Figure 5.4 depicts each participant's ratings split according to the four conditions, revealing remarkable consistency in most cases, albeit with minor variations in the positioning or spread of the data points (e.g., consider listeners 04, 16, 19, or 28). The few listeners with "reversed" response patterns suggest that there may be underlying nuances or individual characteristics influencing their ratings. Specifically, it is noteworthy that for only three listeners (10, 21, 24), condition B exhibited lower ratings than condition A, and for just one listener (10), condition D showed lower ratings than condition A. Conditions D and C displayed the most variability in their relative positioning, with four listeners demonstrating notably lower ratings for condition D (pause + deceleration) compared to Condition C (pause only), which remains unaccounted for.

It is worth mentioning that the behaviour of listener 10 appears somewhat perplexing and challenging to explain, aside from potential idiosyncratic factors or variations in motivation. Nevertheless, this listener exhibited an average response time and provided accurate responses to the distractor items, and therefore cannot be excluded from the sample.

Our experiment provides valuable insights into prosodic boundary perception in Czech and aligns with previous findings in the field. Notably, our study reaffirms the significance of durational cues in shaping the perception of boundary strength. Listeners consistently rated the presence of a pause (condition C) as indicative of a more pronounced boundary compared to the absence of a pause (condition A), thus reinforcing the idea that pauses play a crucial role in prosodic boundary perception (e.g., Männel, Schipke & Friederici, 2013; Yang et al., 2014). In contrast to the evident contribution of pauses, our results suggest that final deceleration alone (condition B) does not enhance boundary perception to a similar degree, echoing previous research that highlights the variable contribution of final deceleration across different languages and contexts (see especially Holzgrefe-Lang et al., 2016). Interestingly, the combination of prosodic cues in condition D (pause + final deceleration) did not yield distinct boundary perception ratings compared to condition C (pause alone), replicating the finding of Yang et al. (2014). This result is consistent with the notion that combining multiple prosodic cues does not necessarily lead to a cumulative effect on boundary perception.

However, it is important to acknowledge several potential limitations of our experiment. We employed a relatively small set of 24 target items, each presented in one condition only. This decision was made to prevent participants from rating identical items multiple times and was also practical, as a more extensive experiment would have taxed the listeners too much. Future research with a larger sample of participants would be advantageous, especially considering the need for proper balancing of conditions across listeners. Moreover, while previous researchers showed that listeners are sensitive to the strength of a boundary based on different levels of the acoustic cues (e.g., de Pijper & Sanderman, 1994), our experiment did not manipulate the size of the prosodic parameters functioning as boundary cues. Instead, we worked with the original values in the recordings, such as a specific pause duration or final lengthening value. A new experiment will be needed for examining whether listeners produce higher boundary strength ratings when pause duration or final deceleration are manipulated to be more pronounced.

Finally, it is crucial to recognize that prosodic boundaries can be influenced by a diverse array of cues, including melodic contours and speech rate. Due to the ex-

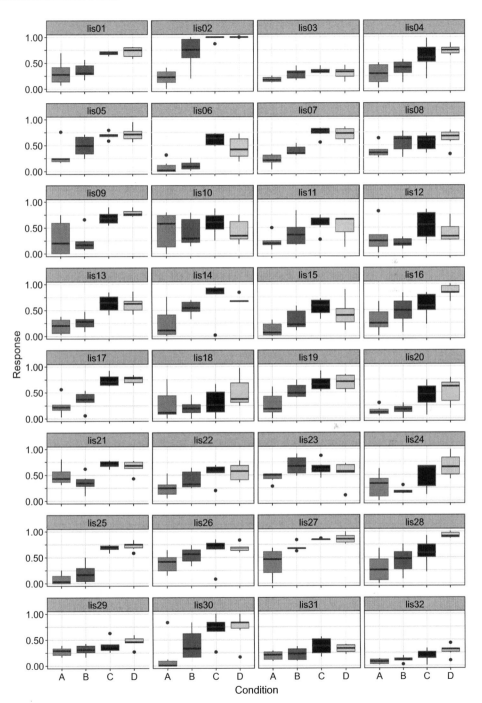

Figure 5.4: *Responses to target items split by individual listeners. A = no cue retained, B = lengthening, C = pause, D = pause + lengthening; 0 = "very tight", 1 = "very loose" connection.*

clusion of these cues in our study, it may not fully capture the intricate nature of prosody in natural speech perception. Therefore, subsequent experiments should aim to investigate the interplay of various prosodic cues to provide a more comprehensive understanding of prosodic boundary perception in Czech, as well as other languages.

5.3 PROSODIC PHRASING AND COGNITION

This section deals briefly with the interplay between prosodic phrasing and language cognition. We start with an inquiry into the ontological status of prosodic phrases – do they represent tangible linguistic entities, or are they constructs of descriptive convenience? This question was partially addressed already in Section 2.3, and we will provide new perspectives here. Subsequently, our focus shifts towards investigating the human brain's capacity to perceive and utilize prosodic phrasing as a cognitive tool, with an emphasis on discerning any cognitive benefits that may be associated with prosodic phrasing. Finally, Section 5.4 introduces an empirical study on this topic involving Czech listeners.

5.3.1 NEUROLINGUISTIC CORRELATES OF PROSODIC PHRASING

Steinhauer, Alter and Friederici (1999) published an important study that introduced the concept of a 'Closure Positive Shift' (CPS) to the field. Employing event-related brain potentials (ERPs), their study illuminated how listeners promptly utilize acoustic cues to prosodic boundaries during speech processing, resulting in a notable positive shift in brain potentials precisely at phrase boundaries. The authors claim that this shift reflects the 'closure' of a prosodic phrase: even in cases of syntax-prosody mismatch, the prosodic interpretation of the processing took precedence, with acoustic features exerting more influence than syntax.

Moreover, the CPS appears to be the brain's response to the presence of a prosodic boundary, rather than merely a reaction to the interruption of the speech stream at the boundary. Even when pauses were deliberately removed from the material, the CPS persisted. The authors suggest that this brain component is linked to the process of structuring the incoming speech signal: "The CPS may be associated with processes that serve to structure the mental representation of the speech signal and to prepare the further analysis of subsequent input. It seems that, at least for the sentences used in the present study, the CPS enables monitoring of prosodically driven parsing decisions long before the syntactically disambiguating element [...] is encountered." (Steinhauer et al., 1999: 195).

The discovery of CPS has reverberated through subsequent studies, where researchers have explored new dimensions of this phenomenon. For instance, Pannekamp, Toepel, Alter, Hahne and Friederici (2005) investigated varying degrees of delexicalization. They created four types of material, ranging from (i) conventional sentences to (iv) hummed utterances devoid of discernible words, with intermediary stages involving (ii) sentences in which lexical words were randomly substituted with meaningless pseudo-words and (iii) sentences composed entirely of pseudo-words. In each case, a stimulus with one prosodic boundary was compared to a stimulus with two prosodic boundaries. The results revealed a corresponding number of CPSs (one or two) across all conditions, regardless of how much lexical information was preserved. This evidence led the authors to assert that "the component is exclusively relying on pure prosodic information" (Pannekamp et al., 2005: 414).

A separate line of inquiry centres on the acoustic cues necessary (or sufficient) for triggering a CPS. As discussed in Section 5.1, the perception of prosodic boundaries can exhibit variability contingent upon language and task. Remarkably, the CPS has emerged as a reliable marker of prosodic boundaries in various languages, including German (Pannekamp et al., 2005), English (Pauker, Itzhak, Baum & Steinhauer, 2011), Dutch (Bögels, Schriefers, Vonk, Chwilla & Kerkhofs, 2010) or Swedish (Roll & Horne, 2011), among others. We will limit our discussion here to German, as it has been the focal point of the majority of CPS investigations.

In addition to the work of Steinhauer et al. (1999) and Pannekamp et al. (2005), who established the CPS as an electrophysiological correlate of prosodic boundary processing, an extensive body of research has emerged in the German context encompassing both adult participants and children spanning various age groups. Männel and Friederici (2011) showed that the anticipated brain response associated with the CPS manifests already in 3-year-old children when exposed to natural stimuli with a complete array of acoustic cues. Nonetheless, a nuanced developmental trajectory emerges when considering distinct cue combinations. In the investigation conducted by Holzgrefe-Lang et al. (2016) involving adults, the absence of pauses in the linguistic material did not impede the elicitation of the CPS. Intriguingly, although neither f_0 modulations nor final deceleration triggered the CPS in isolation, such a response materialized when both cues co-occurred. Similarly, Männel et al. (2013) compared 3- and 6-year-olds and found that only the older cohort exhibited the predicted brain response to boundaries devoid of pauses but still featuring f_0 modulations and deceleration. This specific combination of cues was thus insufficient to induce a CPS response in 3-year-olds. Moreover, Männel and Friederici (2016) examined 3-year-old children who listened to utterances with durational cues (pausing and deceleration) either preserved or reduced, while melodic cues were neutralized in both cases. The CPS component appeared in the absence of f_0 cues but not in the absence of both types of cues. Collectively, these ERP studies suggest that in German 3-year-old children rely more on the pause than 6-year-olds or adults.

5.3.2 MEMORY RETENTION AND OTHER COGNITIVE BENEFITS

The effectiveness of communication belongs to one of the central questions in linguistics, and while its direct measurement remains elusive, researchers often turn to participants' performance in various behavioural tasks that reflect the complexity of processing, or to subjective ratings of the speaker's attributes such as competence. In a study comparing human and artificial voices, the overall prosody of an advertising story influenced effectiveness, as human voices were "rated as more effective and achieved a better level of attention and recall with less concentration" than artificial voices (Rodero, 2017: 345). Notably, when prosody served as the distinguishing factor, human narrators induced superior recall of the story's content. This was evaluated by three open-ended questions referring to information from the text. Similar encouraging results were reported by Goldman et al. (2006) and Mira and Schwanenflugel (2013), where narratives endowed with richer prosody or greater melodic variation facilitated better recall. This underscores the global impact of prosody on cognitive performance in recall tasks.

There is an abundance of research testing MEMORY RECALL (recall, recollection, retention) at the local level as well, but unfortunately, the effect was mostly investigated on strings of nouns, numerals or non-words that were unrelated to each other (Baddeley, 1966; Turner & Engle, 1989; Mathy & Feldman, 2012; Kimball, Yiu & Watson, 2019; Savino, Winter, Bosco & Grice, 2020). However, as we emphasized in Chapter 2, the primary structural unit of natural communication is the utterance, and its essential features such as relational links among words are not present in isolated items. This limitation is acknowledged by Kimball and colleagues: "memory for lists of words likely differs from memory for conversational speech in important ways" (Kimball et al., 2019: 7).

That being said, Elmers, Werner, Muhlack, Möbius and Trouvain (2021) investigated the effect of pauses on digit recollection in synthesized speech. They inserted a pause of either 200 ms or 500 ms in duration before one of seven synthesized digits, and the participants' task was to transcribe three missing digits that were on some occasions preceded by the pause. The presence of either type of pause resulted in higher accuracy in the task compared to the no-pause condition, although longer pauses led to better results. These findings resonate with earlier research (Baumann & Trouvain, 2001) which suggested that pronouncing telephone numbers involves marked prosodic grouping, characterized by alternation of accented syllables and the presence of prosodic phrase boundaries, including the pause. The pause thus seems to be important not only for neuro-linguistic planning (Hawkins, 1971) but also for the processing of the contents of utterances and storing of information in the listener's memory (see, e.g., Shipstead, Lindsey, Marshall & Engle, 2014).

Serial digit recollection is in fact an essential tool that enables researchers and clinicians alike to assess working memory capacity (see Conway et al., 2005, for a methodological review). Therefore, it is important to know which factors affect the recall of auditorily presented digits. Using synthesized speech, Frankish (1995) compared three conditions – pauses, intonation, and a combination of pauses and intonation – to examine their impact on participants' recall performance. His findings revealed that pauses and intonation contributed to enhanced recall to a similar extent. Intriguingly, the combination of these prosodic features did not yield further improvements, prompting Frankish to conclude that once prosodic grouping was established (thanks to pauses), intonation failed to offer additional benefits to the task.

Savino et al. (2020) undertook a meticulous replication of the study using naturally produced intonation patterns in the presentation of digit sequences. Addressing various methodological issues from the previous research, their investigation yielded compelling outcomes. Specifically, the condition with regular list contours, characterized by a rising melody at the conclusion of digit triads and a falling melody on the ninth digit, was associated with better recall compared to a pause condition featuring pauses of 310 ms after each triad, accompanied by a flat f_0 contour. Both of these prosodically marked conditions outperformed an ungrouped control condition, as anticipated. Interestingly, there was also an interaction with digit position. The modulated melody substantially bolstered digit recall particularly in positions corresponding to the rising and falling melodic patterns (i.e., the 3rd, 6th, and 9th digits). In contrast, the sequential impact of pauses was less pronounced.

Let us conclude with a study that shifts the focus from isolated word strings to words embedded within complete sentences. In their investigation, Loutrari, Tselekidou and Proios (2018) examined the impact of a culturally specific feature of Greek storytelling prosody – a distinctive blend of falling melody coupled with highly-extended final deceleration, occurring irrespective of stress placement. Words bearing this unique prosodic feature, atypical of everyday speech patterns, were recalled by child participants more often than words with conventional phrase-final prosody. In addition to the type of material, there is a second difference from the studies mentioned above regarding the procedure. Instead of using serial recall, which requires participants to remember digits/words in a specific order, the authors adopted a free recall paradigm. In this approach, participants listened to a randomized set of sentences, some containing the distinctive prosodic feature and others without it. Subsequently, participants were asked to recollect the final words from the sentences.

5.4 EXPERIMENT ON MEMORY RECALL IN CZECH

In this section, we will discuss the results from an experiment that was reported in full already in Volín and Šturm (2023). The main goal of our research was to establish how the absence of pauses in Czech narrated texts affects memory for the lexical content of the narratives. In contrast to Elmers et al. (2021) and others, who inserted pauses of a specific duration to synthesized or naturally produced speech, Volín and Šturm (2023) deleted pauses that occurred naturally in the material. Our expectation was that words from the spoken material will be better recalled when the pausing was left untouched (Pause condition, 'P') than when it was eliminated (No pause condition, 'NP').

5.4.1 MATERIAL AND METHODS

The material comes from our storytelling database (STR) of audiobook narratives as described in Chapter 3. Eight extracts (spoken by 4 women and 4 men) were selected from the corpus; we avoided passages with overly tense atmosphere or dynamic plot to minimize the influence of the topics. As the speakers were professional actors working under the supervision of the audiobook's production team, their prepared speech was fluent, without disturbing dysfluencies and, importantly, with pauses at logical positions only (i.e., corresponding to the syntactic and semantic structure of the texts). Table 5.2 describes the eight extracts in terms of their duration, number of words and number of pauses. Note that, unlike the duration of the extracts, the number of pauses in each text varied somewhat, which may potentially lead to variation in the effect size. However, other differences (e.g., in liveliness of the speakers or in tempo) should not be crucial due to the repeated-measure design comparing the pause and no-pause conditions. All pauses were removed from the extracts in a sound editor in a way that would not introduce any sound artefacts such as sharp cut-offs. No other acoustic cues to prosodic phrasing were manipulated.

Table 5.2: *Description of the narrative extracts used in the test: duration of the two conditions (with and without pauses) in seconds, number of words and number of pauses. Reproduced from Volín and Šturm (2023: 1431).*

Speaker (Text)	Duration with pauses	Duration without pauses	N Words	N Pauses
F1	45.2	37.2	111	13
F2	46.3	37.1	119	14
F3	48.0	41.2	102	19
F4	46.4	34.3	91	15
M1	48.9	35.9	106	17
M2	46.7	38.1	116	15
M3	47.2	36.9	112	23
M4	48.3	37.3	84	18
Mean	47.2	37.2	105.1	16.8
Std. dev.	1.1	1.8	11.5	3.0

We prepared two experimental versions, randomly assigning them to two separate groups of participants. Each participant was presented with half of the stimuli in condition P (featuring pauses) and the remaining half in condition NP (lacking pauses). Our participants, drawn from various philology courses at the Faculty of Arts, Charles University, willingly volunteered for an experiment aimed at exploring the way people remember words. The sample included 24 native speakers of Czech (18 female, 6 male, mean age = 20.4 years). Testing was conducted in small groups (3-4 people at once) so that the participants could fit comfortably into a quiet room and sit at a similar distance from the loudspeakers. The entire session, including the arrival and instructions, spanned approximately 30 minutes.

The procedure encompassed three key steps that were repeated four times:
1. Participants listened to a pair of spoken narrative extracts (P + NP but using different texts). The order of presentation of the conditions was balanced across groups and alternated throughout the session.
2. Participants were furnished with a transcript for the first extract and given a strict 2-minute time limit to complete the 10 missing words.
3. Participants received a transcript for the second extract, again with a 2-minute time constraint.

The imposition of a time limit ensured consistent time allocation across all participants and stimuli, creating a moderate sense of time pressure. The task was deliberately intended to be difficult to prevent ceiling effects. Participants were explicitly instructed to provide a response for each gap in the text, even if they had to rely on guessing. Furthermore, participants were asked to indicate their familiarity with the narrative text, although these narratives were typically unfamiliar to them.

We also collected benchmark data to determine the general predictability of the target words in the written texts, that is, whether it was possible to complete the gaps without listening to the recordings. The evaluation involved 8 volunteers with similar characteristics to our test participants. The results showed that the majority of the words (78.8% out of 80) were highly unpredictable, while only a small fraction (3.8%) exhibited predictability levels over 50%, signifying that at least four participants provided correct guesses for these words. Additionally, there were eight words for which only a single participant correctly guessed the missing word.

5.4.2 RESULTS AND DISCUSSION

The complete results are reported in Volín and Šturm (2023); we will focus here on the main findings only. The success rate was 24.1% (463 recalled words out of 1,920). Table 5.3 summarizes the results according to condition. There were 10 omitted words in each text and each participant completed 40 words in each condition.

Figure 5.5 illustrates that different participants had varying impacts on the overall results. Although we can compare the participants in terms of their overall performance (e.g., participants R23 and R24 performed notably well while R03 and R11 exhibited much poorer recall), it is crucial to understand the extent to which the effect of condition (P, NP) is driven by individual listeners. Figure 5.5 reveals that two thirds of the participants showed the expected pattern of improved performance under the P condition. However, the other participants reversed the expected pattern or showed equal performance under both conditions. Finally, the results can be interpreted from the perspective of experimental texts. Figure 5.6 demonstrates that the effect size varies among the eight texts, with two texts (F3 and M2) yielding unexpected results.

Table 5.3: *The number of words correctly recalled, split by condition (complete data versus average data per participant and text).*

Condition	Words recalled	Words recalled per listener (max. 40)	Words recalled per text and listener (max. 10)
Pause	265 (27.6%)	11.04	3.31
No pause	198 (20.6%)	8.25	2.47

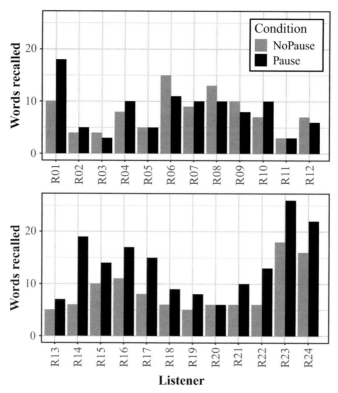

Figure 5.5: *Counts of correctly recalled lexical items by 24 respondents (R01–R24) under two experimental conditions. Reproduced from Volín and Šturm (2023: 1432).*

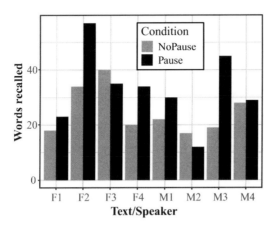

Figure 5.6: *Counts of correctly recalled lexical items in 8 spoken texts under two experimental conditions. Reproduced from Volín and Šturm (2023: 1432).*

The variability in effect size across texts and participants was incorporated into the statistical model that evaluated the significance of the P vs. NP conditions. The nature of the data required fitting a generalized linear mixed model with the Poisson distribution. The count data specified the number of correct responses in each text (thus n = 192, given that 24 subjects filled in 8 texts). One model was constructed with the corresponding random-effect structure, including the by-text and by-participant slopes of the condition effect, and confirmed a significantly better fit of the full model compared to the reduced model ($\chi^2(1)$ = 4.94, p = 0.026). However, as singular fit was returned, we constructed a second, simpler model that included only random intercepts. It yielded smaller p-values ($\chi^2(1)$ = 8.23, p = 0.004), as expected, but it produced almost identical predictions as the random-slope model (see Volín & Šturm, 2023, for more details). The generalizable effect size was approximately 0.5 recalled words per text and listener in favour of P over NP conditions.

Returning to the pre-test benchmark data (Fig. 5.7), we correlated each word's predictability with its behaviour in the experiment, both in terms of recall (left panel) and the effect size (right panel; NP subtracted from P). The analysis offers different insights for the two types of association. On the one hand, there was a significant correlation between predictability and recall rate (r = 0.58, p < 0.001), indicating that words that were easier to guess also had better recall rates after listening. This aligns with expectations and does not pose an issue for the experiment's paired design. On the other hand, predictability had minimal impact on the effect size (r = 0.15, p = 0.172). This finding suggests that the observed effect can be primarily attributed to our manipulations (removing pauses) rather than the predictability of the words.

In conclusion, our experiment strengthens the understanding of pauses as integral components of prosodic structure that play a vital role in enhancing communication effectiveness. Our listeners undeniably derived tangible benefits from the presence of pauses in a memory recall task. We may speculate that when pauses are omitted, per-

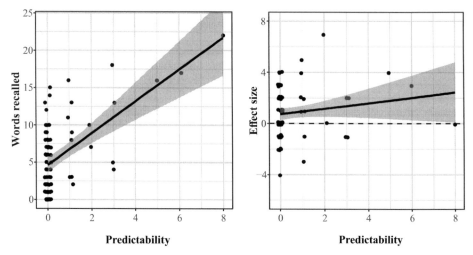

Figure 5.7: *The relationship between predictability of words, based on a pre-test, and recall in the experiment (left) and manipulation effect size (right). Jitter was applied to increase the visibility of overlaid points. Reproduced from Volín and Šturm (2023: 1433).*

ceptual processing is hindered, as the temporal window for further signal processing is limited. However, it is important to temper our initial impression of the effect's magnitude (265 vs. 198 recalled words from the text with and without pauses, respectively); while statistically significant, the effect was not particularly robust. Nevertheless, it should be noted that more substantial effects reported in the literature often originate from highly artificial materials that substantially deviate from typical communicative language use. In contrast, our spoken narrative texts retained their authentic communicative intent.

Our future work must extend beyond pauses and explore the role of other prosodic cues. Savino et al. (2020) have demonstrated that not all forms of prosodic grouping are equally beneficial for speech processing. Groupings demarcated by clear intonation contours, for instance, were associated with superior recall rates compared to those delimited by pauses. Therefore, it is essential to investigate the impact of additional cues such as phrase-final deceleration, amplitude variations, and voice quality changes.

Furthermore, our study assessed short-term memory retention. Helfrich and Weidenbecher (2011) have shown that voice pitch, although not affecting immediate text retention, significantly influences long-term memory. This presents another avenue for future research. Additionally, while our study focused on the memory recall of isolated words, it would be valuable to investigate prosodic effects on comprehension and recall of entire sentences or longer discourse units. Furthermore, exploring these phenomena in different languages and cultural contexts could provide deeper insights into the universality of prosodic cue effects on memory and comprehension.

5.5 CONCLUSION

This chapter has examined the intricate world of prosodic phrase perception. Listeners have a capacity to discern prosodic boundaries even in the absence of lexical or grammatical context, suggesting a substantial degree of independence between the two linguistic domains. We demonstrated that the perceptual process relies on an array of acoustic cues, enabling the identification of prosodic phrases both in controlled laboratory material and in spontaneous speech tokens. The acoustic-perceptual mapping is important not only for identifying boundary locations but also for determining boundary size (strength). For instance, cues such as longer pauses, greater final deceleration, larger f_0 excursions or steeper slopes contribute to the perception of more robust prosodic breaks. An intriguing aspect of this phenomenon lies in the simultaneous engagement of multiple levels of perception, which provides the potential for cues to mutually compensate or interact based on their co-occurrence. Our exploration also highlighted the observed variations across languages and stylistic contexts, indicating that the perceptual weight assigned to each cue is contextually driven. Furthermore, the dynamic nature of speaker behaviour – altering acoustic cue strengths within different contexts – suggests that perception, too, might adapt and rely on diverse cue constellations within the same language. Finally, the perceptual "reality" of the object called prosodic phrases was shown to be supported by neurolinguistic research, and a direct processing or memory benefit was linked to some aspects of phrasing.

6. STOCHASTIC MODELLING OF PHRASE BOUNDARIES

This section presents a summary of recent attempts at an automatic detection of prosodic phrasing – or more precisely, of the boundaries of prosodic phrases – and a subsequent application in speech synthesis; the experiments were conducted by and with our colleagues from the Faculty of Applied Sciences in Pilsen (Kunešová & Řezáčková, 2022; Kunešová & Matoušek, 2023; Volín, Řezáčková & Matoušek, 2021) and used a subset of our newsreading (NWS) corpus (see Chapter 3).

The interest of experts in speech technology and speech processing in prosodic phrase boundaries is not surprising. The knowledge of how prosodic breaks are distributed in speech is beneficial to both dominant tasks of speech technology, namely SPEECH SYNTHESIS and AUTOMATIC SPEECH RECOGNITION. In the former, the knowledge about prosodic phrasing should contribute to synthesized speech sounding more natural, with its prosodic patterns approximating those of human speech. In the latter, correctly identified boundaries will aid in disambiguating sentences such as 'He washed and refuelled the car' (without a prosodic break before the conjunction, the washing would only refer to the 'car', while a boundary would signal that 'he washed himself') and in further stages of processing, for example in syntactic tagging.

While the presence of some prosodic boundaries may be automatically predicted from the orthography, particularly from the usage of commas, this is certainly not always the case and, the other way around, not all commas are reflected in prosodic modifications, as discussed in Section 1.3. For automatic detection of prosodic boundary placement, it is possible to use both lexical and acoustic information; Kunešová and Řezáčková (2022) relied only on acoustic cues in their study. However, their system did not measure a combination of acoustic features such as those analyzed in Section 4.2 – changes of f_0, intensity, duration, or voice quality from one frame to another – to arrive at a probability of prosodic break placement in the given frame. Rather, they used a framework called wav2vec 2.0 (Baevski, Zhou, Mohamed & Auli, 2020), a self-supervised learning framework for training speech representations from raw audio data. This machine-learning model uses a neural network, specifically the Transformer architecture, to learn to 'understand' speech without the need for any labelled data. Put simply, it has no *a-priori* knowledge of the speech signal but learns ('self-supervises' itself) to recognize patterns in it by 'listening' to it. The process is much like what would happen if a person arrived in a foreign country and eventually picked up words and phrases in the ambient language by listening to it. In Kunešová and Řezáčková's (2022) study, the general pre-trained model was fine-tuned for the purpose of classifying audio frames (windows of 20 milliseconds, which is less than a typical speech sound) as to the probability of the frames containing a prosodic break. Of course, the technical aspects are beyond the scope of our description; interested readers are referred to the original research.

Let us examine some of the details of the three studies in more detail. To fine-tune the model, Kunešová and Řezáčková (2022) used our prosodic boundary annotation in the recordings of 12 Czech Radio newsreaders. For this fine-tuning, they used information about both minor (BI3-type) and major (BI4-type) prosodic breaks (see Section 3.5), but their aim was to identify only the major breaks in the recordings. The reasoning behind this choice was the finding from an initial experiment that (major) prosodic breaks are often detected – "falsely", in this case – in places where a minor prosodic break was present. This is not surprising, given that a minor prosodic break is realized using the same acoustic dimensions as a major one, but typically it is realized using only one of them (i.e., either f_0 or duration) and to a weaker degree. Major prosodic breaks were thus assigned a value of 1, and minor breaks the value of 0.5. The results of the modelling showed that adding information about the location of minor prosodic breaks does not improve the performance of boundary detection as such, with the difference in overall accuracy being less than 0.1%. However, a considerably greater percentage of false positives (i.e., falsely identified breaks) corresponded to minor prosodic breaks, as compared to no breaks. In other words, the model was more likely to identify as a major break the frame where a minor break was annotated by human labellers, rather than to place it into a frame where no break at all occurred, which is certainly a positive result. Importantly, as compared to a text-based detection of prosodic breaks, accuracy was higher by one percent using the wav2vec2 approach. From the perspective of speech processing, this is not a negligible improvement, especially given the fact that only 12 speakers and some 42 minutes of speech were used for the fine-tuning.

Figure 6.1 shows a comparison of the expert-annotated prosodic breaks and those automatically predicted using the wav2vec2 system on an exemplary 15-second stretch of speech. A great deal of agreement can be observed in the figure: only one major prosodic boundary identified by human listeners was detected by the system with a probability lower than 0.5 (at approximately 5 seconds). The figure also shows two false positives (around 4.1 and 10.0 seconds), where the probability of boundary presence was estimated as higher than 0.5, but this did not correspond to human expert perception. All remaining peaks are below the 0.5 threshold in accordance with auditory perception.

In the follow-up study, Kunešová and Matoušek (2023) applied the information about prosodic phrasing in a text-to-speech (TTS) system. Their objective was to see whether this enriched prosodic representation results in greater naturalness of the synthesized speech, as perceived by human listeners. The model described above was used to predict prosodic boundary placement in a large corpus of speech of approx-

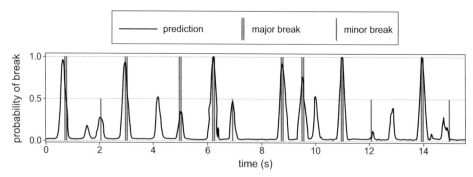

Figure 6.1: *Comparison of human annotation (major and minor breaks indicated by double and single grey lines, respectively) and automatic prosodic break detection (adapted from Kunešová & Matoušek, 2023: 4834).*

imately 14 hours, with two newsreaders (one male and one female). Local maxima identified by the wav2vec 2.0 model (that is, the highest probabilities of boundary presence) were assigned to the end of the nearest word within 100 ms. The authors converted the probability values to two scales: a four-level scale essentially corresponded to the ToBI annotation as used by the human experts (scores 0–3; referred to as P4), and a finer ten-level scale (with scores 0–9; called P10). The higher the number on each scale, the stronger the break identified by the wav2vec2 system; an example of a prediction is illustrated in Figure 6.2.

Subsequently, the authors trained three variants of a neural speech synthesis model (i.e., a system based on deep neural networks, DNNs): (i) P4 and (ii) P10, where the information about phrase boundaries was used, and (iii) a baseline system (P0) with no such additional information. In total, 16 sentences were synthesized for each of the two target speakers using each system variant.

In the next stage of the study, a preference listening test was compiled using the synthesized sentences. In this paradigm, listeners indicated which of the two sentences – differing in the synthesis variant – they preferred. In this listening test, they were specifically instructed to indicate whether the two sentences were identical or whether one was better concerning the quality and naturalness of prosody and intonation. The results of the listening test indicated that, overall, the enriched system containing prosodic boundary information outperformed the baseline P0 system, with approximately 40% of the P4- or P10-synthesized sentences preferred over the baseline. Listeners did not prefer either variant in about 25% to 30% of the sentences, and the same applied to the preference for the baseline variant. Again, the authors point out that the training database of 42 minutes is rather small; it is conceivable that

Figure 6.2: *Example of the P4 and P10 prediction of prosodic break (adapted from Kunešová & Matoušek, 2023: 4835).*

if all our data – the entire newsreading corpus, as well as the storytelling and poetry reciting corpora – are used for fine-tuning the detection of phrase boundaries and the subsequent prediction in synthesized speech, the output from the synthesis system will be even better.

Let us turn to the last study. It was mentioned at the beginning of this section that lexical information (i.e., the written text) may also be used to predict the location of boundaries of prosodic phrases. That was the objective of the study by Volín, Řezáčková and Matoušek (2021): they aimed at finding to what extent another transformer-based neural network can predict phrase boundaries, using a system which was trained on written transcripts and not on audio data. The Text-to-Text Transfer Transformer (known as T5) model was trained to use a sequence of words in a sentence as input and transform it into a sequence which consists of the sentence with predicted phrase boundaries; such models are also known as sequence-to-sequence (seq2seq) models.

The authors conducted three experiments with the T5 model. In the first, they fine-tuned the pre-trained system to create a general phrasing model on a large amount of laboratory speech data; these were extensive texts of recordings from six speakers which were used for the creation of the ARTIC text-to-speech synthesis system developed in Pilsen. This modified T5 system yielded very high accuracy in phrase boundary detection – more specifically, the authors provided a performance score which incorporates all four possible outcomes of a signal detection task: *true positives* (correctly identified boundaries) and *true negatives* (locations where the system correctly does not place a break), *false positives* (incorrectly placed breaks) and *false negatives* (prosodic breaks "missed", not detected by the system). In this first experiment, the false outcomes amounted only to 3%, and the performance score of 90% may be regarded as very high.

In the second experiment, the general model was tested on the 12 newsreaders from the NWS corpus: the aim was to see whether phrase breaks predicted by the system matched those identified by a human expert annotator in the newsreaders' speech. The comparison yielded slightly lower scores as compared to the first experiment; the greatest change consisted in higher false negatives. In other words, the system failed to identify – based on the written text of the news – some of the realized boundaries. The most important boundaries, which are predictable from the text based on punctuation, were detected successfully and the true positive and true negative scores were quite high. However, prosodic breaks which are not as transparent in the written version were not predicted, resulting in the performance score of 68%.

The objective of the third experiment was therefore to fine-tune the general T5 system from the first experiment with the annotations from the NWS corpus. As in the studies reported above, the NWS corpus itself would have been insufficient for training an entirely new phrasing model, but it was used to adapt the one obtained in the second experiment and to predict boundaries in this corpus. A "leave-one-out" procedure was applied, in which eleven speakers were chosen for such adaptation, and boundaries were predicted in the text of the twelfth speaker; this procedure was repeated for all the twelve texts. The fine-tuning, performed on only a small corpus, improved the performance significantly, as shown by the overall performance score of 76%. Specifically, the false negative rate dropped considerably (from 50% to 33%), though at the cost of a small increase in the false positive rate.

In a more detailed analysis, the authors examined the syntactic-semantic makeup of the sentences and focused specifically on the mismatches between human (recording-based) annotation and automatic (text-based and recording-adapted) prediction. The main categories of mismatches are summarized in Table 6.1. However, it must first be pointed out that a missed prosodic boundary does not automatically mean that the system made an "error"; prosodic boundary placement is not categorical in the "either correct or false" sense. The table therefore also provides information, in the second data column, whether the phrasing predicted by the adapted T5 system would have been acceptable – specifically, whether no semantic ambiguities would result and whether the given prosodic phrases would not be excessively long. In fact, the dataset contains several instances where the predicted phrasing of a sentence was preferable to the solution adopted by the specific newsreader.

Table 6.1: *The most frequent syntactic-semantic categories of mismatched prosodic boundaries (see text; adapted from Volín, Řezáčková & Matoušek, 2021: 769).*

Category	Total	Acceptable	Missed	Added	Other
Subject-predicate division	146	115	109	23	14
Post-positioned attribute	85	64	70	4	11
Sentence-initial adverbial	71	51	55	4	12
Grammatical object	45	33	35	4	6
Numerals	36	22	25	2	9
Conjunction 'a' or 'i'	35	29	19	9	7
Apposition	32	21	21	7	4
Verb/Copula Ellipsis	19	14	16	1	2

It can be seen from the table that more than 30% of the mismatched cases correspond to the prosodic division of the sentence subject and predicate: the system "missed" 109 such divisions, as illustrated by examples (18) and (19). Notice that these subjects are quite short, and the predicted absence of the boundary would still be acceptable, as was the case with most mismatches in this category. Acceptability would be considerably lower in example (20), where joining the subject part of the sentence (*pacientka teplické nemocnice*) with the remainder of the phrase would result in an unusually long phrase.

(18) Další podrobnosti ‖ zatím nejsou k dispozici ‖
     Further details ‖ are not yet available ‖

(19) Pozornost ‖ je ale upřena hlavně na italského kandidáta Rocca Buttiglioneho ‖
Attention ‖ is focused however mainly on the Italian candidate Rocco Buttiglione ‖
(20) Pravděpodobnost ‖ že by pacientka teplické nemocnice ‖ měla lidskou formu nemoci šílených krav ‖ je podle odborníků mizivá ‖
The likelihood ‖ that the patient of the Teplice hospital ‖ could have the human form of the mad cow disease ‖ is according to experts minimal ‖

On the other hand, the system also predicted 23 breaks in places where none occurred in speech, as exemplified on the first break at the beginning of sentence (21); all of these may be regarded as acceptable.

(21) Nový předseda vlády ‖ by mohl zaujmout tvrdší postoj ‖ k demokratickému hnutí disidentky ‖ On-Šan Su-Tij ‖
The new prime minister ‖ may adopt a harsher attitude ‖ toward the democratic movement of the dissident ‖ Aung San Suu Kyi ‖

The large number of mismatches in the subject-predicate division was to be expected, since Czech does not allow for these constituents to be separated by a comma, even in cases when they are complex (i.e., consist of more words). Therefore, many such prosodic breaks will be realized without a corresponding cue in the written texts, which makes it more difficult for the model to predict.

The second most frequent category included cases where an attribute (which typically appears before the noun in Czech) followed the noun. Prosodic boundary insertion is not uncommon in such cases, especially to avoid excessively long phrases, but many of these instances were missed by the T5 system; again, however, most of the resulting phrases would have been acceptable without the boundary, as shown in (22).

(22) Uvedla to ČTK s odvoláním na operačního důstojníka ‖ centra tísňového volání ‖
It was mentioned by CPA (Czech Press Agency) with reference to an operation officer ‖ of the emergency call centre ‖

A similar tendency was revealed in the third most frequent category: as in English, an adverbial in Czech may appear sentence-initially, though this occurs much more frequently in English. Unlike in English, however, such adverbials are not separated by a comma in Czech, which is the likely reason why many of these instances were missed by the automatic text-based prediction; an example of a missed prosodic break is provided in (23). However, there were also cases when the T5 system predicted a phrase break where none occurred in the given newsreader's speech, as shown at the beginning of sentence (24).

(23) Do dnešního dne ‖ ji shlédlo přes sto sedmdesát tisíc návštěvníků ‖
Until this day ‖ it has been seen by over a hundred and seventy thousand visitors ‖
(24) Do snížené sazby ‖ se má vrátit například vstupné do muzeí | na historické památky ‖ ...
Into the lower rate ‖ what should return is for example entrance fees into museums ‖ historic monuments ‖ ...

The study by Volín et al. (2021) shows that automatic prediction based on the deep structure of texts is comparable with human annotation of recordings. Importantly, most of the mismatches did not result in sentences which would be semantically ambiguous. As with the previously reported studies in this section, a small adaptation dataset proved to be adequate to fine-tune the automatic system and significantly improve its performance. It remains to be seen whether the improvement would continue with a larger adaptation set.

REFERENCES

Aasland, W. A., & Baum, S. R. (2003). Temporal parameters as cues to phrasal boundaries: A comparison of processing by left- and right-hemisphere brain-damaged individuals. *Brain and Language*, 87(3), 385–399.

Abercrombie, D. (1964). *Elements of general phonetics*. Edinburgh University Press.

Armstrong, L. E., & Ward, I. C. (1926). *A handbook of English intonation*. Heffer.

Auer, P. (1996). On the prosody and syntax in turn-continuations. In E. Couper-Kuhlen & M. Selting (Eds.), *Prosody in conversation* (pp. 57–100). Cambridge University Press.

Austin, J. L. (1962). *How to do things with words*. Clarendon Press.

Baddeley, A. D. (1966). Short-term memory for word sequences as a function of acoustic, semantic and formal similarity. *Quarterly Journal of Experimental Psychology*, 18(4), 362–365.

Baevski, A., Zhou, Y., Mohamed, A., & Auli, M. (2020). wav2vec 2.0: A framework for self-supervised learning of speech representations. *Advances in Neural Information Processing Systems*, 33, 12449–12460.

Banse, R., & Scherer, K. R. (1996). Acoustic profiles in vocal emotion expression. *Journal of Personality and Social Psychology*, 70(3), 614–636.

Bates, D., Mächler, M., Bolker, B., & Walker, S. (2015). Fitting linear mixed-effects models using lme4. *Journal of Statistical Software*, 67, 1–48.

Baumann S., & Trouvain, J. (2001). On the prosody of German telephone numbers. In *Proceedings of Eurospeech 2001*, 557–560.

Beckman, M. E. (1992). *Stress and non-stress accent*. De Gruyter Mouton.

Beckman, M. E. (1996). The parsing of prosody. *Language and Cognitive Processes*, 11 (1/2), 17–67.

Beckman, M. E., & Ayers Elam, G. (1997). *Guidelines for ToBI labelling, version 3*. The Ohio State University Research Foundation, Ohio State University.

Beckman, M. E., & Pierrehumbert, J. B. (1986). Intonational structure in English and Japanese. *Phonology Yearbook*, 3, 255–309.

Biber, D., & Conrad, S. (2009). *Register, genre, and style*. Cambridge University Press.

Blevins, J. (2006). Syllable typology. In K. Brown (Ed.), *Encyclopedia of language and linguistics* (Vol. 12) (2nd ed., pp. 333–337). Elsevier.

Boersma, P., & Weenink, D. (2023). *Praat: Doing phonetics by computer* (version 6.3.10). Retrieved from http://www.praat.org.

Bögels, S., Schriefers, H., Vonk, W., Chwilla, D. J., & Kerkhofs, R. (2010). The interplay between prosody and syntax in sentence processing: The case of subject- and object-control verbs. *Journal of Cognitive Neuroscience*, 22(5), 1036–1053.

Bolinger, D. (1964). Around the edge of language: Intonation. *Harvard Educational Review*, 34(2), 282–296.

Bořil, T., & Skarnitzl, R. (2016). Tools rPraat and mPraat: Interfacing phonetic analyses with signal processing. In P. Sojka, A. Horák, I. Kopeček & K. Pala (Eds.), *Proceedings of 19th International Conference on Text, Speech and Dialogue* (pp. 367–374). Springer International Publishing.

Browman, C. P., & Goldstein, L. M. (1995). Gestural syllable position effects in American English. In F. Bell-Berti & R. J. Lawrence (Eds.), *Producing speech: Contemporary issues. For Katherine Safford Harris* (pp. 19-33). AIP Press.
Brown, G., & Yule, G. (1983). *Discourse analysis*. Cambridge University Press.
Bühler, K. (1934). *Sprachtheorie. Die Darstellungsfunktion der Sprache*. Fischer. Translated by D. F. Goodwin & A. Eschbach (2011) as *Theory of language. The representational function of language*. John Benjamins.
Campione, E., & Véronis, J. (2002). A large-scale multilingual study of silent pause duration. In *Proceedings of Speech Prosody 2002*, 199-202.
Carlson, R., Hirschberg, J., & Swerts, M. (2005). Cues to upcoming Swedish prosodic boundaries: Subjective judgment studies and acoustic correlates. *Speech Communication, 46*, 326-333.
Chafe, W. L. (1987). Cognitive constraints on information flow. In R. S. Tomlin (Ed.), *Coherence and grounding in discourse* (pp. 21-51). John Benjamins.
Chafe, W. L. (1988). Linking intonation units in spoken English. In J. Haiman & S. A. Thompson (Eds.), *Clause combining in grammar and discourse* (pp. 1-27). John Benjamins.
Chafe, W. L. (1992). Information flow in speaking and writing. In P. A. Downing, S. D. Lima & M. Noonan (Eds.), *The linguistics of literacy* (pp. 17-29). John Benjamins.
Chafe, W. L. (1994). *Discourse, consciousness, and time (The flow and displacement of conscious experience in speaking and writing)*. University of Chicago Press.
Chafe, W. L. (2001). The analysis of discourse flow. In D. Schiffrin, D. Tannen & H. E. Hamilton (Eds.), *The Handbook of discourse analysis* (pp. 673-687). Blackwell.
Cho, T. (2016). Prosodic boundary strengthening in the phonetics–prosody interface. *Language and Linguistics Compass, 10*(3), 120-141.
Cho, T., & Keating, P. (2009). Effects of initial position versus prominence in English. *Journal of Phonetics, 37*, 466-485.
Chomsky, N., & Halle, M. (1968). *The sound pattern of English*. Harper & Row.
Clifton, C. Jr., Carlson, K., & Frazier, L. (2002). Informative prosodic boundaries. *Language and Speech, 42*(2), 87-114.
Cohen, A., Collier, R., & t'Hart, J. (1982). Declination: Construct or intrinsic feature of speech pitch? *Phonetica, 39*, 254-273.
Conway, A. R. A., Kane, M. J., Bunting, M. F., Hambrick, D. Z., Wilhelm, O., & Eagle, R. W. (2005). Working memory span tasks: A methodological review and user's guide. *Psychonomic Bulletin & Review, 12*(5), 769-786.
Corretge, R. (2022). Praat Vocal Toolkit. Retrieved from https://www.praatvocaltoolkit.com.
Cruttenden, A. (1997). *Intonation* (2nd ed.). Cambridge University Press.
Cutler, A. (2005). Lexical stress. In D. B. Pisoni, & R. E. Remez (Eds.), *The handbook of speech perception* (pp. 264-289). Blackwell Publishing.
Daneš, F. (1957). *Intonace a věta ve spisovné češtině* [Intonation and sentence in standard Czech]. Československá akademie věd.
de Pijper, J. R., & Sanderman, A. A. (1994). On the perceptual strength of prosodic boundaries and its relation to suprasegmental cues. *Journal of the Acoustical Society of America, 96*(4), 2037-2047.
Duběda, T. (2011). Towards an inventory of pitch accents for read Czech. *Slovo a slovesnost, 72*(1), 3-12.
Easterday, S. (2019). *Highly complex syllable structure: A typological and diachronic study*. Language Science Press.
Eimas, P. D. (1999). Segmental and syllabic representations in the perception of speech by young infants. *Journal of the Acoustical Society of America, 105*(3), 1901-1911.
Ellis, N. (2003). Constructions, chunking, and connectionism: The emergence of second language structure. In C. J. Doughty & M. Long (Eds.), *The handbook of second language acquisition* (pp. 63-103). Blackwell.
Elmers, M., Werner, R., Muhlack, B., Möbius, B., & Trouvain, J. (2021). Evaluating the effect of pauses on number recollection in synthesized speech. In *Proceedings of 32nd Conference Elektronische Sprachsignalverarbeitung (ESSV, 21)*, 298-295.
Eskenazi, M. (1993). Trends in speaking styles research. In *Proceedings of Eurospeech 1993*, 501-509.

Firbas, J. (1992). *Functional sentence perspective in written and spoken communication*. Cambridge University Press.
Frankish, C. (1995). Intonation and auditory grouping in immediate serial recall. *Applied Cognitive Psychology, 9*(7), 5–22.
Fujisaki, H. (1983). Dynamic characteristics of voice fundamental frequency in speech and singing. In P. F. MacNeilage (Ed.), *The production of speech* (pp. 39–47). Springer-Verlag.
Fox, A. (2000). *Prosodic features and prosodic structure: The phonology of suprasegmentals*. Oxford University Press.
Gårding, E. (1998). Intonation in Swedish. In D. Hirst & A. Di Cristo (Eds.), *Intonation systems* (pp. 112–130). Cambridge University Press.
Ghitza, O., Giraud, A.-L., & Poeppel, D. (2013). Neuronal oscillations and speech perception: Critical-band temporal envelopes are the essence. *Frontiers in Human Neuroscience, 6*, 340.
Gibbon, D. (2015). Speech rhythms – modelling the groove. In R. Vogel & R. van de Vijver (Eds.), *Rhythm in cognition and grammar. A Germanic perspective* (pp. 54–80). De Gruyter.
Giegerich, H. (1992). *English phonology: An introduction*. Cambridge University Press.
Goldman, S. R., Meyerson, P. M., & Cote, N. (2006). Poetry as a mnemonic prompt in children's stories. *Reading Psychology, 27*, 345–376.
Gordon, M. (2016). *Phonological typology*. Oxford University Press.
Gordon, M., & Roettger, T. (2017). Acoustic correlates of word stress: A cross-linguistic survey. *Linguistics Vanguard, 3*, 1–11.
Greene, R., Cushman, S., Cavanagh, C., Ramazzani, J., & Rouzer, P. (2012, 4th Ed.). *Princeton encyclopedia of poetry and poetics*. Princeton University Press.
Grepl, M., & Karlík, P. (1986). *Skladba spisovné češtiny*. Státní pedagogické nakladatelství.
Grossberg, S. (2003). Resonant neural dynamics of speech perception. *Journal of Phonetics, 31*(3–4), 423–445.
Gussenhoven, C., & Rietveld, A. C. M. (1988). Fundamental frequency declination in Dutch: testing three hypotheses. *Journal of Phonetics, 16*, 355–369.
Hála, B. (1956). *Slabika, její podstata a vývoj* [Syllable, its nature and development]. Československá akademie věd.
Halberstam, B. (2004). Acoustic and perceptual parameters relating to connected speech are more reliable measures of hoarseness than parameters relating to sustained vowels. *ORL, 66*, 70–73.
Hallé, P. A., & Christia, A. (2012). Global and detailed speech representations in early language acquisition. In S. Fuchs, M. Weirich, D. Pape & P. Perrier (Eds.), *Speech planning and dynamics* (pp. 1–27). Peter Lang.
Halliday, M. A. K. (1967). *Intonation and grammar in British English*. Mouton.
Halliday, M. A. K., & Matthiessen, C. (2014). *Halliday's introduction to functional grammar* (4th ed.). Routledge.
Hanson, H. M., & Chuang, E. S. (1999). Glottal characteristics of male speakers: Acoustic correlates and comparison with female data. *Journal of the Acoustical Society of America, 106*(2), 1064–1077.
Hapka, H. (2023). *Tematicko-rematické členění výpovědi a amplituda řečového signálu v českých narativech* [Information structure of utterances and the amplitude of speech signal in Czech narratives]. Unpublished MA thesis, Faculty of Arts, Charles University, Prague.
Hawkins, P. R. (1971). The syntactic location of hesitation pauses. *Language and Speech, 14*, 277–288.
Hejná, M., Šturm, P., Tylečková, L., & Bořil, T. (2021). Normophonic breathiness in Czech and Danish: Are females breathier than males? *Journal of Voice, 35*(3), 498.e1–498.e22.
Helfrich, H., & Weidenbecher, P. (2011). Impact of voice pitch on text memory. *Swiss Journal of Psychology, 70*(2), 85–93.
Hillenbrand, J., Cleveland, R., & Erickson, R. (1994). Acoustic correlates of breathy vocal quality. *Journal of Speech and Hearing Research, 37*, 769–778.
Hirst, D., & Di Cristo, A. (1998). *Intonation systems: A survey of twenty languages*. Cambridge University Press.
Holzgrefe-Lang J., Wellmann, C., Petrone, C., Räling, R., Truckenbrodt, H., Höhle, B., & Wartenburger, I. (2016). How pitch change and final lengthening cue boundary perception in German: Con-

verging evidence from ERPs and prosodic judgements. *Language, Cognition and Neuroscience, 31*(7), 904–920.

Hoskovec, T. (2010). Věta a výpověď ve znakovém pojetí jazyka [Sentence and utterance in the sign concept of language]. In A. Bičan, J. Klaška, P. Macurová & J. Zmrzlíková (Eds.), *Karlík a továrna na lingvistiku – Prof. Petru Karlíkovi k šedesátým narozeninám* (pp. 190–199). Host.

Hyman, L. M. (2011). Does Gokana really have no syllables? Or: what's so great about being universal? *Phonology, 28*(1), 55–85.

Jankowski, L., Astésano, C., & Di Cristo, A. (1999). The initial rhythmic accent in French: Acoustic data and perceptual investigation. In *Proceedings of 14th ICPhS*, 257–260.

Janota, P., & Palková, Z. (1974). The auditory evaluation of stress under the influence of context. In M. Romportl & P. Janota (Eds.), *Acta Universitatis Carolinae – Philologica: Phonetica Pragensia, 4* (pp. 29–59). Charles University.

Jassem, W. (1952). *Intonation of conversational English (educated Southern British)*. Nakł. Wrocławskiego Towarzystwa Naukowego.

Jeon, H. S., & Nolan, F. (2013). The role of pitch and timing cues in the perception of phrasal grouping in Seoul Korean. *Journal of the Acoustical Society of America, 133*(5), 3039–3049.

Joos, M. (1968). The isolation of styles. In J. Fishman (Ed.), *Readings in the sociology of language*. Mouton.

Jusczyk, P. W., & Derrah, C. (1987). Representation of speech sounds by young infants. *Developmental Psychology, 23*(5), 648–654.

Kimball, A. E., Yiu, L. K., & Watson, D. G. (2019). Word recall is affected by surrounding metrical context. *Language, Cognition and Neuroscience, 35*(3), 383–392.

Kohler, K. J. (1966). Is the syllable a phonological universal? *Journal of Linguistics, 2*(2), 207–208.

Kohler, K. J. (2018). *Communicative functions and linguistic forms in speech interaction*. Cambridge University Press.

Kolář, R., Plecháč, P., & Říha, J. (2013). *Úvod do teorie verše* [Introduction to verse theory]. Akropolis.

Kühnert, B., & Nolan, F. (2006). The origin of coarticulation. In W. J. Hardcastle & N. Hewlett (Eds.), *Coarticulation* (pp. 7–30). Cambridge University Press.

Kunešová, M., & Matoušek, J. (2023). Neural speech synthesis with enriched phrase boundaries. In: *Proceedings of Interspeech 2023*, 4833–4837.

Kunešová, M., & Řezáčková, M. (2022). Detection of prosodic boundaries in speech using wav2vec 2.0. In: P. Sojka, A. Horák, I. Kopeček & K. Pala (Eds,), *Text, Speech, and Dialogue. TSD 2022. Lecture Notes in Computer Science, vol 13502* (pp. 377–388). Springer.

Labrune, L. (2012). Questioning the universality of the syllable: Evidence from Japanese. *Phonology, 29*(1), 113–152.

LaCroix, A. N., Blumenstein, N., Tully, M., Baxter, L. C., & Rogalsky, C. (2020). Effects of prosody on the cognitive and neural resources supporting sentence comprehension: A behavioral and lesion-symptom mapping study. *Brain and Language, 203*, 104756.

Ladd, D. R. (1983). Peak features and overall slope. In A. Cutler & D. R. Ladd (Eds.), *Prosody: Models and measurements* (pp. 39–52). Springer-Verlag.

Ladd, D. R. (1986). Intonational phrasing: the case of recursive prosodic structure. *Phonology Yearbook, 3*, 311–340.

Ladd, D. R. (1988). Declination "reset" and the hierarchical organization of utterances. *Journal of the Acoustical Society of America, 84*(2), 530–544.

Ladd, D. R. (2000). Bruce, Pierrehumbert, and the elements of intonational phonology. In M. Horne (Ed.), *Prosody: Theory and experiment* (pp. 37–50). Springer.

Laver, J. (1994). *Principles of phonetics*. Cambridge University Press.

Lehiste, I. (1975). The phonetic structure of paragraphs. In A. Cohen & S. G. Nooteboom (Eds.), *Structure and process in speech perception* (pp. 195–206). Springer-Verlag.

Lenth, R. V. (2023). *emmeans: Estimated Marginal Means, aka Least-Squares Means*, v. 1.8.8. Retrieved from https://CRAN.R-project.org/package=emmeans.

Liberman, M., & Pierrehumbert, J. (1984). Intonational invariance under changes in pitch range and length. In M. Aronoff & R.T. Oehrle (Eds.), *Language sound structure* (pp. 157–233). MIT Press.

Lieberman, P. (1967). *Intonation, perception, and language*. MIT Press.

Lin H.-Y., & Fon, J. (2009). Perception of temporal cues at discourse boundaries. In *Proceedings of Interspeech 2009*, 808–811.

Lin, P. (2018). *The prosody of formulaic sequences*. Bloomsbury Academic.

Lindblom, B. (1990). Explaining phonetic variation: A sketch of the H&H theory. In W. J. Hardcastle & A. Marchal (Eds.), *Speech production and speech modelling* (pp. 403–439). Springer.

Local, J., & Walker, G. (2005). Methodological imperatives for investigating the phonetic organisation and phonological structures of spontaneous speech. *Phonetica, 62*, 120–130.

Loutrari, A., Tselekidou, F., & Proios, H. (2018). Phrase-final words in Greek storytelling speech: A study on the effect of a culturally-specific prosodic feature on short-term memory. *Journal of Psycholinguistic Research, 47*, 947–957.

Machač, P., & Skarnitzl, R. (2009). *Principles of phonetic segmentation*. Epocha Publishing.

Maddieson, I. (2013). Syllable structure. In M. S. Dryer & M. Haspelmath (Eds.), *The world atlas of language structures online*. Max Planck Institute for Evolutionary Anthropology. https://wals.info/chapter/12.

Männel, C., & Friederici, A. D. (2011). Intonational phrase structure processing at different stages of syntax acquisition: ERP studies in 2-, 3-, and 6-year-old children. *Developmental Science, 14*(4), 786–798.

Männel, C., Schipke, C. S., & Friederici, A. D. (2013). The role of pause as a prosodic boundary marker: Language ERP studies in German 3- and 6-year-olds. *Developmental Cognitive Neuroscience, 5*, 86–94.

Mathesius, V. (1939). O tak zvaném aktuálním členění věty [About the so-called functional sentence perspective]. *Slovo a slovesnost 5*(4), 171–174.

Mathesius, V. (1943). O srozumitelnosti a působivosti mluveného slova v rozhlase [About comprehensibility and impresivness of the spoken word on the radio]. *Slovo a slovesnost, 9* (2-3), 138–145.

Mathy, F., & Feldman, J. (2012). What's magic about magic numbers? Chunking and data compression in short-term memory. *Cognition, 122*, 346–362.

Ménard, L. (2013). Sensorimotor constraints and the organization of sound patterns. In C. Lefebvre, B. Comrie & H. Cohen (Eds.), *New perspectives on the origins of language* (pp. 257–278). John Benjamins.

Mira, W. A., & Schwanenflugel, P. J. (2013). The impact of reading expressiveness on the listening comprehension of storybooks by prekindergarten children. *Language, Speech, and Hearing Services in Schools, 44*, 183–194.

Nekvapil, J. (1987). Historiografické poznámky k problematice věty a výpovědi [Historiographic notes on the matter of sentence and utterance]. *Jazykovedný časopis, 38*(1), 60–76.

Nespor, M., & Vogel, I. (1983). Prosodic structure above the word. In A. Cutler & R. Ladd (Eds.), *Prosody: Models and measurements* (pp. 123–140). Springer-Verlag.

Nespor, M., & Vogel, I. (1986). *Prosodic phonology*. Foris Publications.

O'Connor, J. D. (1980). *Better English pronunciation* (2nd ed.). Cambridge University Press.

O'Connor, J. D., & Arnold, G. F. (1973). *Intonation of colloquial English* (2nd ed.). Longman.

O'Connor, J. D., & Trim, J. L. M. (1953). Vowel, consonant, and syllable – A phonological definition. *Word, 9*(2), 103–122.

Ogden, R. (2001). Turn transition, creak and glottal stop in Finnish talk-in-interaction. *Journal of International Phonetic Association, 31*, 139–152.

Ogden, R. (2010). Prosodic constructions in making complaints. In D. Barth-Weingarten, E. Reber & M. Selting (Eds.), *Prosody in interaction* (pp. 81–104). John Benjamins.

Ogden, R. (2012). The phonetics of talk in interaction – Introduction to the special issue. *Language and Speech, 55*(1), 3–11.

Ogden, R. (2024). Phonetic perspectives on interaction: Ways of observing speech. In J. D. Robertson, R. Clift, K. Kendrick & C. Raymond (Eds.), *Handbook of Research Methods in Conversation Analysis*. Cambridge University Press.

Oller, K. D. (2000). *The emergence of the speech capacity*. Psychology Press.

Ondráčková, J. (1954). O mluvním rytmu v češtině [About speech rhythm in Czech]. *Slovo a slovesnost, 15*, 24–29 and 145–157.

Palková, Z. (1994). *Fonetika a fonologie češtiny* [Phonetics and Phonology of Czech]. Karolinum.
Palková, Z., Veroňková, J., Volín, J., & Skarnitzl, R. (2004). Stabilizace některých termínů pro fonetický popis češtiny v závislosti na nových výsledcích výzkumu [Stabilization of selected terms for the phonetic description of Czech based on new research results]. In T. Duběda (Ed.), *Sborník z Konference česko-slovenské pobočky ISPhS* (pp. 65–74). Faculty of Arts, Charles University.
Palková, Z., & Volín, J. (2003). The role of F0 contours in determining foot boundaries in Czech. In *Proceedings of 15th ICPhS*, 1783–1786.
Pannekamp, A., Toepel, U., Alter, K., Hahne, A., & Friederici, A. D. (2005). Prosody-driven sentence processing: An event-related brain potential study. *Journal of Cognitive Neuroscience, 17*, 407–421.
Patterson, D., & Ladd, D. R. (1999). Pitch range modeling: Linguistic dimensions of variation. In *Proceedings of 14th ICPhS*, 1169–1172.
Pauker, E., Itzhak, I., Baum, S. R., & Steinhauer, K. (2011). Co-operating and conflicting prosody in spoken English garden path sentences: Evidence from event-related potentials. *Journal of Cognitive Neuroscience, 23*, 2731–2751.
Petrone, C., Truckenbrodt, H., Wellmann, C., Holzgrefe-Lang, J., Wartenburger, I., & Höhle, B. (2017). Prosodic boundary cues in German: Evidence from the production and perception of bracketed lists. *Journal of Phonetics, 61*, 71–92.
Petřík, S. (1938). *O hudební stránce středočeské věty* [The musical aspect of Central Bohemian sentence]. Faculty of Arts, Charles University.
Pierrehumbert, J. B. (1980). *The phonology and phonetics of English intonation* (PhD dissertation). MIT/Indiana University Linguistics Club.
Pike, K. L. (1945). *The intonation of American English*. University of Michigan Press.
Pike, K. L. (1947). *Phonemics*. University of Michigan Press.
Pollák, P., Volín, J., & Skarnitzl, R. (2007). HMM-based phonetic segmentation in Praat environment. In *Proceedings of XIIth "Speech and Computer – SPECOM 2007"*, 537–541.
Price, J. M. (2021). *The perceived effect of pause length and location on speaker likability and communicative effectiveness*. MA thesis, Department of Communication Disorders, Brigham Young University. Retrieved from https://scholarsarchive.byu.edu/etd/9144.
R Core Team (2020). *R: A language and environment for statistical computing* (version 4.0.3). Vienna: R Foundation for Statistical Computing. Retrieved from https://www.rproject.org.
Raphael, L. J. (2005). Acoustic cues to the perception of segmental phonemes. In D. B. Pisoni & R. E. Remez (Eds.), *The handbook of speech perception* (pp. 182–206). Blackwell Publishing.
Remez, R. E. (2021). Perceptual organization of speech. In J. S. Pardo, L. C. Nygaard, R. E. Remez & D. B. Pisoni (Eds.), *The Handbook of Speech Perception* (pp. 3–27). Wiley Blackwell.
Renský, M. (1960). Funkce slabiky v jazykovém systému [Function of the syllable in the language system]. *Slovo a slovesnost, 21*(2), 86–95.
Roach, P. (1991). *English phonetics and phonology: A practical course* (2nd ed.). Cambridge University Press.
Roach, P. (2009). *English phonetics and phonology: A practical course* (4th ed.). Cambridge University Press.
Rodero, E. (2017). Effectiveness, attention, and recall of human and artificial voices in an advertising story. Prosody influence and functions of voices. *Computers in Human Behavior, 77*, 336–346.
Roll, M., & Horne, M. (2011). Interaction of right- and left-edge prosodic boundaries in syntactic parsing. *Brain Research, 1402*, 93–100.
Sacks, H., Schegloff, E. A., & Jefferson, G. (1974). A simplest systematics for the organization of turn-taking for conversation. *Language, 50*(4), 696–735.
Savino, M., Winter, B., Bosco, A., & Grice, M. (2020). Intonation does aid serial recall after all. *Psychonomic Bulletin & Review, 27*, 366–372.
Scherer, K. R. (2003). Vocal communication of emotion: A review of research paradigms. *Speech Communication, 40*, 227–256.
Scott, D. R. (1982). Duration as a cue to the perception of a phrase boundary. *Journal of the Acoustical Society of America, 71*(4), 996–1007.
Shipstead, Z., Lindsey, D. R., Marshall, R. L., & Engle, R. W. (2014). The mechanisms of working memory capacity: Primary memory, secondary memory, and attention control. *Journal of Memory and Language, 72*, 116–141.

Shue, Y. (2020). *VoiceSauce: A program for voice analysis*, v1.37. Retrieved from http://www.phonetics.ucla.edu/voicesauce/.

Shue, Y.-L., Keating, P., Vicenik, C., & Yu, K. (2011). VoiceSauce: A program for voice analysis. In *Proceedings of 17th ICPhS*, 1846–1849.

Skaličková, A. (1954). K otázce podstaty slabiky [Concerning the nature of the syllable]. *Slovo a slovesnost*, 15(1), 19–24.

Skarnitzl, R. (2018). Fonetická realizace slovního přízvuku u delších slov v češtině [The phonetic realization of lexical stress in longer words in Czech]. *Slovo a slovesnost, 79*, 199–216.

Skarnitzl, R., & Hledíková, H. (2022). Prosodic phrasing of good speakers in English and Czech. *Frontiers in Psychology, 13*, 857647.

Skarnitzl, R., & Volín, J. (2019). The effect of durational cues on the reassignment of a syllable in the metrical structure of Czech sentences. In *Proceedings of 19th ICPhS*, 2891–2895.

Sluijter, A. M., & Terken, J. M. (1993). Beyond sentence prosody: Paragraph intonation in Dutch. *Phonetica, 50*, 180–188.

Sluijter, A. M. C., & van Heuven, V. J. (1996). Spectral balance as an acoustic correlate of linguistic stress. *Journal of the Acoustical Society of America, 100*, 2471–2485.

Steinhauer, K., Alter, K., & Friederici, A. D. (1999). Brain potentials indicate immediate use of prosodic cues in natural speech processing. *Nature Neuroscience, 2*, 191–196.

Stetson, R. H. (1951). *Motor phonetics: A study of speech movements in action* (2nd ed.). North-Holland Publishing Company.

Šturm, P., & Bičan, A. (2021). *Slabika a její hranice v češtině* [The syllable and its boundaries in Czech]. Karolinum.

Šturm, P., & Volín, J. (2023). Occurrence and duration of pauses in relation to speech tempo and structural organization in two speech genres. *Languages, 8*, 23.

ten Have, P. (2007). *Doing conversation analysis*. Sage Publications.

Trager, G. L., & Smith, H L. (1951). *An outline of English structure*. Battenburg Press.

Trim, J. L. M. (1959). Major and minor tone-groups in English. *Le Maitre Phonetique, 112*, 26–29.

Trost, P. (1962). Subjekt a predikát [Subject and predicate]. *Acta Universitatis Carolinae – Slavica Pragensia 4*, 267–269.

Turner, M. L., & Engle, R. W. (1989). Is working memory capacity task dependent? *Journal of Memory and Language, 28*, 127–154.

Tylečková, L., & Skarnitzl, R. (2019). The mapping of voice parameters in connected speech of healthy Common Czech male speakers. *Akustické listy, 25*, 10–18.

Umeda, N. (1982). "F0 declination" is situation dependent. *Journal of Phonetics, 10*, 279–290.

van Lancker, D., & Canter, G. J. (1981). Idiomatic versus literal interpretations of ditropically ambiguous sentences. *Journal of Speech and Hearing Research, 46*(1), 64–69.

Volín, J. (2008a). Variabilita neukončujících melodií ve světle shlukové analýzy [Cluster analysis and variability of continuation rises in Czech]. *AUC-Philologica 2007/2*, 173–179.

Volín, J. (2008b). *Downtrends in standard British English intonation*. Hector.

Volín, J. (2009). Extrakce základní hlasové frekvence a intonační gravitace v češtině [Extraction of fundamental frequency and intonational gravitation in Czech]. *Naše řeč, 92*(5), 227–239.

Volín, J. (2019). The size of prosodic phrases in native and foreign-accented read-out monologues. *Acta Universitatis Carolinae – Philologica 2/2019, Phonetica Pragensia XV*, 145–158.

Volín, J., Řezáčková, M., & Matoušek, J. (2021). Human and transformer-based prosodic phrasing in two speech genres. In: A. Karpov & R. Potapova (Eds.), *Speech and Computer, SPECOM 2021. Lecture Notes in Computer Science*, vol 12997 (pp. 761–772). Springer.

Volín, J., & Skarnitzl, R. (2007). Temporal downtrends in Czech read speech. In *Proceedings of Interspeech 2007*, 442–445.

Volín, J., & Skarnitzl, R. (2018). *Segmentální plán češtiny* [Segmental plan of Czech]. Faculty of Arts, Charles University.

Volín, J., & Skarnitzl, R. (2020). Accent-groups vs. stress-groups in Czech clear and conversational speech. In *Proceedings of Speech Prosody 2020*, 695–699.

Volín, J., & Skarnitzl, R. (2022). The impact of prosodic position on post-stress rise in three genres of Czech. In *Proceedings of Speech Prosody 2022*, 505–509.
Volín J., & Šturm, P. (2021). Honouring historical facts: The case of intonational downtrends. In *Proceedings of 4th International Workshop on History of Speech Communication Research*, 63–73. (Vol. 101 of *Studientexte zur Sprachkommunikation*). TUD Press.
Volín, J., & Šturm, P. (2023). The absence of pauses in spoken narratives and memory recall. In *Proceedings of 20th ICPhS*, 1430–1434.
Wells, J. C. (2006). *English intonation: An introduction*. Cambridge University Press.
Werner, R., Trouvain, J., & Möbius, B. (2022). Optionality and variability of speech pauses in read speech across languages and rates. In *Proceedings of Speech Prosody 2022*, 312–316.
Wichmann, A. (2000). *Intonation in text and discourse: Beginnings, middles, and ends*. Longman.
Wickham, H. (2016). *ggplot2: Elegant Graphics for Data Analysis*. Springer-Verlag. Available at: https://ggplot2.tidyverse.org/.
Wray, A. (2002). *Formulaic language and the lexicon*. Cambridge University Press.
Yang, X., Shen, X., Li, W., & Yang, Y. (2014). How listeners weight acoustic cues to intonational phrase boundaries. *PLoS ONE*, 9(7), e102166.
Yoon, T.-J., Cole, J., & Hasegawa-Johnson, M. (2007). On the edge: Acoustic cues to layered prosodic domains. In *Proceedings of 16th ICPhS*, 1017–1020.
Zahorian, S. A., & Hu, H. (2008). A spectral/temporal method for robust fundamental frequency tracking. *Journal of the Acoustical Society of America*, 123(6), 4559–4571.
Zellers, M., & Ogden, R. (2013). Exploring interactional features with prosodic patterns. *Language and Speech*, 57(3), 1–25.
Zellner, B. (1994). Pauses and the temporal structure of speech. In E. Keller (Ed.), *Fundamentals of speech synthesis and speech recognition* (pp. 41–62). John Wiley & Sons.
Zhang, X. (2012). A comparison of cue-weighting in the perception of prosodic phrase boundaries in English and Chinese. PhD dissertation, University of Michigan.

SUBJECT INDEX

A
accent group 35
accenting 16
acoustic dimensions 19
aesthetic function 18
aesthetic sensations 18
affective 11, 15, 23, 44
anacrusis 32, 34, 58
annotation 44
arousal axis 23
automatic detection 130
automatic speech recognition 130

B
boundary cues 110
break indices 45
breath-group 30
building elements 20

C
cadence 20, 21
cepstral peak prominence 86
Closure Positive Shift 118
colon 30
comment 28
complex prosodic phrases 51
conative 11, 15, 21
configurations 20
co-text 16
CPP 86
CPS 118
critical discourse analysis 16

D
deceleration 24, 45, 81, 109
declination 23, 108

declination reset 32
definition by listing 13
definition by negation 13
definition by parallel 13
discourse 15, 29
discourse analysis 16
domain of loudness 19
downstep 23
downtrend 23, 24
duration 19, 24, 81

E
ERP 118
event-related brain potentials 118
explicit subject 98

F
factorial trends 23
false negatives 133
false positives 133
final deceleration 24, 45, 81, 109
final lengthening 24
final lowering 24
foot 34
forensic phonetics 17
formulaic language 26
Fujisaki model 21
functional linguistics 19
fundamental frequency 68

G
genre 23, 30, 40
grammatical function 16

H
hierarchical approach 21
hierarchical organization 26
holistic approach 22

I
illocutionary force 15
implicit 98
indexical function 17
information structure 29
information unit 31
intensity 32, 73, 91
intermediate phrase 33
intonation phrase 33
intonation unit 31
intonational phrase 31

L
language cognition 118
level 20, 22
lexical function 18
linear modelling 21
loudness 19

M
major prosodic phrase 33
meaning 28
melodeme 20
melodic domain 18
melody 19
memory recall 108, 120
memory retention 120
mental processing 11
minor prosodic phrase 33
monosyllabic stress group 61
multi-word units 12

N
nuclear pitch accent 21, 32
nuclear pitch configuration 31

O
operational space 22
orthography 13

P
paragraph 29
paratone 29
pause 53, 110, 120
perceptual cues 19
perceptual process 108
perceptual significance 108
phonoparagraph 29
phrase length 49
pitch range 23
promluvový úsek 30
prosodeme 21
prosodic boundary 32
prosodic domains 18
prosodic events 18
prosodic factors 19
prosodic phenomena 18
prosodic phrase 31
prosodic syntax 22
PSOLA 112

R
register 40
rhythm rule 61
rPraat 68, 73, 80

S
sentence 27
schwa 35
sociophonetic function 17
sociophonetic markers 17
span 22
speech synthesis 13
stress clash 61
stress group 35
style 40
subject-predicate boundary 98, 102
subject-predicate division 134
syllabic nucleus 37
syllable 36
syntax 22, 33, 93

T
tempo 19
temporal domain 19, 80
texts 19
timbre 19
ToBI 20, 33, 45, 132
tone 21
tone group 31
tone languages 18
topic 28
true negatives 133
true positives 133
turn 30
turn-taking 30

U
utterance 11, 14, 26, 28, 45

V
voice quality 32, 86, 108, 126

W
wav2vec2 system 131